Written
in Rain
New & Selected Poems
1985–2000

M. L. Liebler

Tebot Bach
Huntington Beach ✿ 2000

ISBN: 1-893670-09-0
Library of Congress Catalogue Card No: 00-131212

Manuscript typed by Kathleen Zamora for the YMCA of Metropolitan Detroit
Cover design: Melanie Matheson
Layout & book design: Alan Berman
Front cover and section photographs: Roland Harrison
Author photo: John Sobczak, Lorien Studio

Printed in Canada

Tebot Bach
20592 Minerva Lane
Huntington Beach, California 92646 USA

For Shane & Shelby who gave me back America—
and for Edward Sanders for teaching me its history again.

Foreward

In an ever-materialistic and self-centered world it is a pleasant surprise to find a man who chooses to not only write poems as an occupation but to strive to include all other poets and points of view. This book of 15 years of poetry tells us much about not just the poet but the land and the people he lives with and in. M. L. Liebler not only attempts to describe and relate his feelings and insights but to draw the audience into his vision and make them aware of who and what they are. His poetry, like his life, is about "community," something we will spend the next century trying to rediscover. This book will help us in our quest.

M. L. best describes his goals in the poem "Allen Ginsberg's Dead." The poem helps us to understand this eternal human occupation, his occupation: the writing of poems; and to see and hear the beauty of his style and mind:

> *But, isn't that what poetry is all about?*
> *Images speaking to the unspeakable*
> *In our dreams as we lie awake in our sleep?*
>
> *And, now, because I've shared this poem*
> *With all of you, we are forever connected*
> *All of our bones together*
> *Side by side in the rich graveyard*
> *Soil of poetry and life.*

M. L.'s attempts to "connect" people through the beauty and insight of his poems give us all that sense of "community" that makes life worth living.

—Country Joe McDonald

Acknowledgments

The author wishes to publicly thank the following publications where many of these poems and stories first appeared:

Exquisite Corpse, Drum Voice Review, Gargoyle, The Paterson Literary Review, Rattle: Poetry for the 21st Century, The Prague Literary Journal, The Christian Science Monitor, Wordswright, The Big Scream, Long Shot, The University of Hong Kong Literary Journal, Poetry Motel, The Lilliput Review, The University of Windsor Literary Review, The Red Brick Literary Review, Pig Iron Journal, The Great Midwestern Literary Review, The Heartlands Today Journal, Nexus Literary Journal of Wright State University, The Underground Review, The Black Cat Literary Review, The MacGuffin Literary Journal, Artforum Journal of North Dakota, San Fernando Poetry Journal, The Sweet Anne Review, The Burning World Literary Review, The Mermaid Tavern Lit Review, The Bullhead Review, Transmog, The Bridge Literary Journal, Chance Review, The Detroit Sunday Journal, C&G Publications, The Great Lakes Review, Mimesis Review, Brix Literary Review, The Broadside Press's Broadside Series, Broken Street Christian Literary Magazine, The Christian Poet, Cold Drill Review & CD Series, The Cranbrook Literary Review, The Detroit News, The Graffiti Rag Literary Journal, Howling Dog Literary Review, The Metro Times, The New York Press, ONTHEBUS, Quadra-Project Calendar & Postcard Series, The Red Eye Incident: Investigative Poetry Collection, Relix Music Magazine, L'Auteur Literary Review, Slipstream Literary Magazine and Cassette Series, The South End Newspaper, Triage: A Journal of New Writing, WindowPane, Wired Literary Quarterly.

Anthologies

Identity Lessons (Viking-Penguin), *A Gathering of Poets* (Kent State University Press), *Abandoned Automobile: Poetry from Detroit* (Wayne State University Press), *Revival: Poetry from Lollapalooza* (Manic-D Press), *The Worker Writers' Labor Writings* (UAW Publications), *Baseball: An Anthology* (University of Illinois Press), *Labor Pains: Labor Poets* (Ridgeway Press), *CCNY's Poetry in Performance Anthology, Coffeehouse Poetry Anthology* (Bottom Dog Press), *The Canadian Wayzgoose Anthology of International Writing* (University of Windsor Press), *In The West of Oreland Poetry Anthology*

Special Thanks

Pam, Kathy Zamora, Mifanwy Kaiser, Larry Smith, Kali Tal, Edward Sanders, W. D. Ehrhardt, Alicia Ostriker, Shirley Geok-lin Lim, Anca Vlasopolos, Stellasue Lee, Amiri Baraka, Jayne Cortez, Richard Tillinghast, Al Kooper, Country Joe McDonald, Jorma Kaukonen, Stewart Francke and Magic Poetry Band members Jim Carey, Ted W. Nagy, Brigitte Knudson, Jason Shinder, Jan Waters, Larry Kameya, and all the good people at Wayne State University, The YMCA of Metropolitan Detroit and The YMCA of the USA. I am especially grateful to all of my students at Wayne State University.

"And it was at that age . . . Poetry arrived
in search of me. I don't know, I don't know where
it came from, from winter or a river.
I don't know how or when,
no, they were not voices, nor silence,
but from a street I was summoned,
from the branches of night . . .
there I was without a face
and it touched me."

Pablo Neruda

"I don't believe it's all for nothing."

Robbie Robertson

Contents

Breaking the Voodoo
Parkville Publishing: 1990

Deliver Me (Christian Poems)
Ridgeway Press: 1991

Stripping the Adult Century Bare
Viet Nam Generation, Inc. & Burning Cities Press: 1995

Brooding the Heartlands
Bottom Dog Press: 1998

Written in Rain: New Poems

Written
in Rain
New & Selected Poems
1985–2000

Whispers by the Lawn:

Volume I
(Exit Back)

Fish

My words are like fish
Twisting under whitecaps,
Where hearts are seaweed
And gills are rocks.

My words rush to shore,
With the tide,
And smash upon the beach
And quickly retreat,
Leaving letters
Belly-up
With bloated eyes staring
Half sand and half water.

In My Spring

I may not dream
Again
About the county ditch
Or about the banana spider's web
Of decent despair.

I may not move
Myself
To the bottom
Of the promiscuous bush
Of serenity.

I may never, again, pluck simple berries
Taste backyard mud
Stick my shoes in fresh rain water
Drag them across laundryroom tiles.

I may never feel warm
Again
while teetering back and forth
Along a suspended wish
Across a latent smile
Stretched over a clothesline in despair.

I cannot press green grass
And corner dust
Up against my cheeks.
I will never again lean on plaster beams
Pick rivets
Yell love
Hold my boyhood leash
Dream wet laughter
And spell the future out
Amongst the fields and passions.

I can no longer
Cry
In my mother's afternoon lap.

My Old Neighborhood

Catching mad falling leaves
In our broken bottle bellies.

Hurling scarred cigarette butts
From atop aging tree forts
In haunted oak trees.

Blessed are those moments
When the future sleeps.

Whispers by the Lawn

Long ago,
In the blue-green stalk
Of a blade of grass,
Hung the broken pieces
Of an eye
That winked
At a past of
Dust and joy.

Tormented by the season's seed
And angelic whispers,
All the children melted
Back
Into the sun.

As an ode
To faithless charm
And repenting lawns,
The future comes
Like an injured animal
To die.

All Our Fathers

When all our fathers
Sink their bones
Deep
Into the worm earth,
The stalking, painless shadow
Will scream.

The lightening green earth
Will waltz the moon
Into surface shadows
Of domestic stress.

Time will lapse the skull
While running thoughts
Will evaporate the path.

When we move our fathers
Out of their bones,
Vengeance will cripple the distance
And malice charm
Will cross the focus.

Fish Dinner

They sat
Across from each other.
Stained glass formed
In their eyes
Like spider web reflections.
Catholicism splashed
Within their souls.
They had some talk.
They had some dinner.
They had memories,
As big as rain clouds,
Hanging over their heads
Making their bodies frail
And their tongues soft.

They were old.
But they were somebody's treasures.
Maybe like old baseball cards,
Or like dress shoes
Worn once and stored.
There was evidence of pain
In their tired eyes,
But that is to be expected

Whenever skin sags on bones,
Men look forward
To fish dinners
And small talk
In hopes of exaltation.

The Picture of a Man

Here, in this picture, is
The shape of a man
Holding his dreams
Tight between flat fingertips.

As he steps in front
Of a mirror to think,
A shadow slowly ebbs
Up over
his shoes
And past
His knees.

Here, in this picture, is
A man being eclipsed
By a twilight
That is as dark as sharks
Swallowing the pale blue lights
of his soul.

Heat

I took my spirit walking
Into the shale
Of a brown-gray moon.

Transient was the night
Free to move
and to slowly etch itself
Into the backs of earthworms
That are our backyards.

I walked through the night
And inward towards
The thin veins of the sun
And over the weak bones of the clouds.

I felt a season
That stuck, hot,
Against the tight skin
Of summer.

Pulling and picking,
The wind harvested my spirit
Into a million and one clusters
Of different ideas
That eased my eyelids
In the face of heat.

Midwest #1

Crossing from a simple touch
Into the richness of a black night,
I drop dreams
Like dead birds
Off of the backs of sleeping trains.

Africa

for Fela

There was a decision made
When, first, I was
A rhythm and sensation moving
Towards an unfocused destination.

Somehow, someway I had to produce
Just so I
Could evaporate back
Into a raindrop
Left to hang
From a bright, green leaf
The size and texture
Of an elephant's ear.

From the moss
My soul oozed
Like a hydra dream
Or more like an amoeba
Chasing itself—
Circle within circle.

I was once a heartbeat
Buried deep
In the bare mud.
I was fluid and porous.
I was, myself,
Pulsating and changing,
Convoluting and flowing,
Furrowing time
In the same way time
Cuts the river deep.
I am the river!
In my blackness—
In my whiteness—
Lilly-assed and loved.

14

There was a decision made
When, first, I was
A rhythm and sensation moving
Towards an unfocused destination.

Son of Laughter

for Bert Williams

Last night,
In a dream,
Bert Williams came to me—
He parted clouds with
Rolling eyes,
Face burnt cork,
Lips spread white.
His head was held up
In the harness
Of a minstrel's vision.

Across a curtain
In a comedic angle,
The moon hung
And looked like
A ragweed shadow
As it pricked laughter
From vanity's ruse.

Bert could snap applause
From the many guilty trees,
And later, he pulled smiles
With defined words
From broken origins.

In 1922
He was laid to rest
In a Harlem night
Of incense and new born jazz.

It all adds up
To create the portrait ghost
Of patience
Of struggle
Of the King of Comedy
Who came to visit me
In the blackness of my sleep.

The Funeral

It was black.
I turned, quickly,
To notice my mother
Slip,
Mysteriously,
Into the sky.

A crack,
Like an incision, opened
And up she went
In fearless movement—
Far, far away.

The next thing I knew
I was surrounded by kissing aunts
With very pale, thin lips
And by shaky, shaking uncles' hands.
It was so cold
and so black.
There was no music,
Only the old songs
In my head
Around my dreams.

The festival of death
Seemed to protrude
Into my mother's serenity
Like Moses and the stone—
Like Jesus and the wood—

However
Now,
Sometime later,
All I recall
Is chit-chat, lunchmeat, and Gershwin.

Exit Back

There's a lot
Of waiting and sickness
Balled-up
And strained through
Each of our souls.
It's like pushing
All of our hurt
Through the eye
Of a needle.

There's always pain
Waiting with sickness
To cover us
While we sleep.

We count breaths.
We count heartbeats.
We count sins.
And each of these things
Reminds us
Just how mortal
And just how
Expendable
We really are!

Every day and every night
Is savage
For taking us out
Back of our souls
And whipping us senseless
And torturing our sleep
Deep in the caverns
Of our dark, dark thoughts.

We are sick.
And we are waiting,
As we die in our hearts,
To exit back.

Whispers by the Lawn

Volume II

In a Window

One hot summer night
I sat in the window
With the fan blowing
Ice on my back.
I listened to the neighbor
Scream bloody murder
At his four children,
Of which two are adopted.
I folded my arms over
My face like an eclipse
As the heat
From the night and
From his words
Burned the earth down
To the thick layers of the dead ghosts
That are forever buried
In the steam of the mud.

As the moon passed
From one side of the morning,
His words became tears
And his children became cracked mirrors.
With each breath he drew in from
The steamy underside
Of his deferred sleep.

He whimpered to himself
Until sometime close to 6:00 a.m.
That he had lost his will.
He felt as though the future
Had asked him to exist
As long as he could exit by sunrise.

It now appears
That he has lost himself
Forever.
He seems to realize
That he will go on
As just another man.

Unemployment

I've stood in line.
I've stood on line
Long enough to know
What assistance is.

I've taken time out
of my life
To get money
To get food
To continue on
With my life.

I've been in and out doors
That revolve and twist men's souls
When they discover that
Their insides
Can be turned outside
By this musty, desperate world.

I've spent sweaty nights
In smoke-filled dreams
Created by a fire
That burns deep
In my hollow soul.
My fucking hollow soul
That I've bared
In bread lines—
In soup lines—

I've stood in lines
With my father
And I've watched anguish crawl
Over his face
Like earthworms
Over sidewalks
After hard thunderstorms.

I know about some
Goodtimes and some hardtimes,

But I've only seen goodtimes
Through the reflections
In other men's eyes
And not in my father's.

The river run,
The river run deep
And keeps silent
With a raging undercurrent.

This world is
an endless line,
An unbroken line,
In an unbroken cycle.

I've stood in lines.
I've stood on lines.
The river run silent.
The river run deep
Beneath a long line
Of men and their work.

Dog Days

I slid over the belly
Of the cat night
Like a cloud greasing the sky
For rain.

In the quiet corners
Of the earth's soul
Where mud is pushed
Hard
Against the strained light
Of a passing moon,
Many events appear
Destined to polish
The surface
Of enchantment and chance.

But I'll be damned
If something doesn't always happen,
When memories tire
And when the future dances
Off of the backs
Of sleeping dogs
On hot summer days.

The Twilight Blues #1

Twilight sickness
Creeping around broken bottles
While toothpicks exhaust suspense
And sweat.

Murky, meandering streams
Of ash can burdens
Fill wailing cries
with tortured whispers.

It all makes me
Wish that I
Could lean on nature
Like oppression leans on the blues.

Vietnam
The Asshole Blues
(prelude to "Rusted Clock")

My parents died
Several years ago.
I don't always spend
A lot of time anymore
Thinking about them,
But when I do,
It hurts—
It hurts very badly.

Vietnam ended
Several years ago.
I don't always spend
A lot of time anymore
Thinking about it.
But when I do,
It hurts—
It hurts very badly.

My soul will ache.
Blood runs thru my bones
Meshing red with white bone china.
I think about the pain
In my youth
That held me together
Like the night holds a fever.
I think about the neighbor boy
Whose bones were left
In the mud fields of Vietnam.
I think about Johnson
And Nixon, later, Kicking
Our white, suburban asses
Back down the throats
Of our parents who
Kicked our asses out
Like the birds kick their own

Out after they've fallen
From the nest.

Kicking white asses!
Killing black asses
Like they was no asses
At all!
O I got them asshole blues—
Them assholes blues
Again!

I told those bastard people
That we was comin back
To kick *their* asses
And they told me
That we was going to,
"In the future, you
  just wait and see,
  You'll grow up!
  Cause you'll be readin ads
  In business journals,
  And grown ups listen
  To the media
  Not no Jimi Hendrix flag burnin bastard
  Like you was!"
O I got them asshole blues,
Them assholes blues again.
O they burnin my ass yea!
Like the Hemorrhoids of a nation
I hate war like segregation.
I've got no relation
Without those gels
My ass does swell.
But I got the burns
Deep in my pants
And it feels like the ants
Have taken this hill
Hell!
I got them asshole blues again.

And the neighbor boy
Ain't comin home

No more.
He's in the mud
Cut like a lamb
Sacrificed in Vietnam
That neighbor boy
Ain't comin back
No more!
No more!
No more!

Rusted Clock

Within the whispers
Of slivering seconds,
As bygones are bygones,
The truth breathes under
The river of tense, stale revolution.

To the faithful,
The movement represents a release
Of fear
Through the exorcism
Of their sins.

Through the barrios
Of grass and mud huts,
Where clocks rust
As their gears eat air,
Pain squeezes on and on
Through the cracks of one hundred,
Or more, years.

The pain reflects off the tribal cuts
Across the faces of the men and the women,
But more than that, it moves
In force over
The tender dreams of children.

Children that should be rubbing soil
Through their gentle fingers
And not through their soft, young bones.
Children that should be pulling breath
From the innocent fields
While laughing and tapping with insects.

Children that should never have learned to pull triggers
In the crotch of the nightmare jungle,
Amongst the rain and banana trees.

Enough is enough
As bygones are bygones,
When our backs are up against
The ancient spikes
Of broken moments
That stab our open hearts with whispered hope.

Listen to the Stars

SHHH!!!
QUIET!!!
LISTEN to the stars.
They talk soft.
Don't they talk soft?
Listen as their beams
Pass lightly over
The lawns in our neighborhoods
Of silence.

Behind the doors,
The seemingly broken doors,
Folded into the prayers,
The seemingly broken prayers,
Is the silence of GOD
Rising slowly above
The stars' beams
To create a soft sense
Of peace within Us
And the world's wicked soul.

I Read a Book

In the future,
The changes will come
From under the heart
And beyond an equator
That will be known
As the soul.

At that time,
We will see
A more detailed shadow in,
Let's call it,
The spirit.

In some, there will be
A swelling, while in others
There will be
A deepening of the veins
And an expansion of the muscles.

As these spirits fill with blood,
They will produce a concept of self
Awareness and of Faith,
And we will call all
Of this the future.

This will all take place
After the evil, dried weeds
Are cleared away from
Our bruised and battered pasts.
We will rejoice when
We realize that
life, as we knew it, was
Only a map
Leading us home
To our eternity.

I Learned How to Pray

In a dark corner
Of my soul,
Hidden beneath a
Rockbed of mercy,
I learned how to pray.

First, I folded
My knees behind my eyes.
Then I bent them
Back into my skull.

I asked Jesus
To save me.
I think I said, "Save my doggone soul!"
Because I was weaned on rockabilly.

I felt His presence
Fold around me.
He was invisible,
But He was strong.
I felt terror being released
From every cell in my body.
I saw my spirit
Slide out of my side
And float up
Into the ceiling of the city.
My two eyes became stars
In the night,
And for one second
I saw GOD
And learned how to pray.

Take Me Back into the Earth

I'd like to imagine
All of us as rocks,
Waiting to have life
Breathed deep into our soft souls.

I'd like to see
Us all lined up
Like birds on a wire.
I once saw birds
Lined on a wire
Hiding in my closet.
They looked like bumps
On a thin vein
Leading to the outside
Of my dreams.

I've always liked the challenge
That new roads and trails bring,
But they are often rough to travel
Alone I feel
Like a bird made
Out of rock
Just waiting
For the vein to dry and crumble
Down into the earth's shy surface
Taking me back
Into the ground
Like ashes to ashes
And dust to dust.

Dead Art!

for John Lennon & Thelonious Monk

Somewhere
In the rustic canons
Of fortune and fame
Lies
The dizzying breath
Of ancient skill
and contemporary art.

With each sweep
Of religious sorrow
And penitent chant,
Art dies
And swims down
"A lazy river"

to rest
and regroup

Breaking the
Voodoo

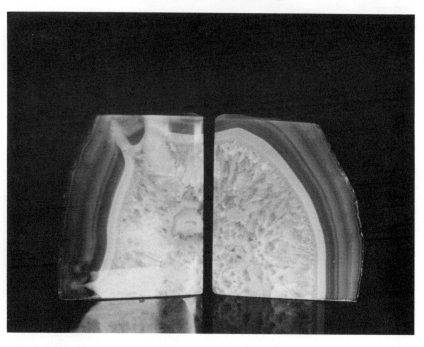

The Jazz

for Faruq Z. Bey

The touch is soft
And meaningful
And fast
Like jazz
Uptown
In sweat
In tears
In hard driving notes
That break our opportunities.
High
High
The jazz
The jazz
Can you dig what's happening here?
The blowing future barking
Us back to the dog houses
Of our present lamp,
And the jazz
The jazz
It beats and polishes
Everything
Every damn thing
Let it talk soft
And slow
Let us say no words—
Just listen to the jazz—
To the jazz.

When the Mentally Retarded Live
in Your Family

We all have secret
Scent that we hide
Right here
Behind our ear

We struggle
To keep it
Right in place
Hidden
But sometimes
When the sky is blue
When the world seems
To love
When life is a flower
Our scent releases itself.

When this happens
The first thing we do
Is lie
About its presence
But its release changes
Our style
Our lives
And our history.

We love our scent
Because it is from us
But we hate to share it
Because it is all we have
Of our softness and truth.

When the Mentally Retarded Live
in Your Neighborhood

The scent stinks!
It isn't behind your ear,
On the back of your neck or
In the middle of your soul.
It's simply not yours.

You didn't see it—
Didn't smell it
And certainly didn't birth it.
It's not yours!

When darkness came,
And you did what you do
To create new life,
You weren't there.
You were drunk—
You were on vacation—
You were out of commission
Because it isn't yours.

You decided, all by yourself, that it was an "it."
Since it isn't yours
You feel no obligation
To see it
To touch it.
To talk to it.
It's not yours.

It belongs to the neighborhood.
The neighbors must share it.
When the world is a flower
They love it.
While you cut your grass,
You are too busy for it.

It loves you!
But it's not yours!!

My Dad's a Prick!

We gotta problem here!
Kids today are pissed off
Because for the first time
In the history of the world,
Parents are hipper than their kids.

They don't know
How to deal
With this newest phenomenon.
They're pissed off
And we can't help it.

They're used to jerking
Mom and Dad around
And up and down,

But now—No Go!
They hear from older cousins
And friends of cousins' friends
That once it was different.
Once, Moms and Dads were jerks.
They went to wars.
Supported presidents.
Shopped at supermarkets,
Long before 7/11's.
They only ate pizza once, maybe twice, a month.

Now, it's pizza once or twice a week—
Sometimes a day.
No more war!
No more support for presidents!
No more shopping for things
That can't be put in a microwave!

We gotta real problem here!
Our children are even listening
To subpar music:
Madonna, Beastie Boys, Run DMC.
You have to admit

That's a long way from Bob Dylan.

I think what we have here
Is a real chance to communicate,
But my son thinks
I'm a prick.

Now I Understand
(How My Mother Died)

They worked her
Into the mud.
They beat her
Head into the sinks
And into the tiles
Of their workhouses.
They slit her,
Belly up,
And dressed her
Like a deer
After the almighty hunt.

Now, I understand how
My mother died.
In the lie
That surrounded her labor,
Her honest-honest labor
That boiled production
And brought it all to a head
For their profit
And for her dead spirit.

Drained of blood,
And no one to cover
Her white, white bones,
And no one to wipe her brow,
Over her sunken eyes.
This is how
My mother died.
"Honest work for honest pay."
This lie is white hot,
But it won't burn
Forever.
In her breast
Forever.

Now my mother flashes
Before my eyes,

Before my eyes,
Working her ass
Her ass off
To maintain her room
Her little, little room
In a project
On the eastside of Detroit
1950s
Just after my birth.

"Honest pay for honest work."
This lie can't live
Forever.
Forever.
Forever.

And when she died,
And when her A.D.C. checks stopped,
And when they didn't have to give
Her money,
And when they missed her labor,
Her cheap-cheap labor,
Then they remembered
Her part of their lie.
It keeps

Forever.
Forever.
Before my eyes
She flashes
She smolders
In their kitchens
In their ovens
In her sweat and labor.
It won't live
It won't live.
It won't
Live.
It lives
It won't live.
It lives.
It lives.
It lives.
Forever.

Somewhere in America
After Vietnam/Before Central America
for Pamela

Somewhere in America
A mother buries her head
Deep into her hands
And closes her eyes.

Somewhere in America
I stand in a city
Rubbing my fingers
Over a name in granite.

Closing my eyes
It feels like rubbing
My beard early in the morning
But that will grow.
This name will never breathe
Again the mother remembers
Her reason for burying
Her head deep
Into the pocket of a lie.

She doesn't want to think
About freedom.
She has lost her rights
To raise her boy.

Another day in America.
Another day in a city.
Somewhere there are too many
Who have lost
And who will never have
The freedom to win.

Malcolm X Knew This (Before His Birth)

If you are
Going to dismantle this
Whole thing take it
Down tear it apart
Strip by strip away
From the nerves of the bones
That make up the bodies
And cage the souls
Of this world that counts
On order hoping
For futures as wide
And as deep as the veins
That hold the blood that creates
A moving pulse that beats
Freedom pumping the pasts
In one end
And out the other then
Be prepared to die
When it all goes when the break-
Down cracks at the seams
The frantic will panic and rip
The whole thing strip
It bleed it cold
Pump out generation after
Generation the future lies
Distorting the soul's
Pulse beating itself
Dead right down
Dead to the nerve

Keep the Bantu Drinking

In the heat
Of another South African night,
At the edge
Of the Jungle,
They're keeping
The Bantu drunk.

Giving them liquor
Keeping them dreamy,
Hazy. Keeping them
Lying lazy.

Drink is the king
Of the new jungle, and beer halls
Are his dens,
As the future becomes
Moss and sleep.

Keep the Bantu drunk
In South Africa.
Keep people everywhere
Less than sober—
Less than awake!

Give them beer.
Give them whiskey.
Give them all
As much as they can
Drink. They believe
In the power
Of liquid. It keeps
Them low and away.

It makes them whisper
Instead of shout.
It gives them
Disease for body and soul.
It turns away
The spirit

Of the family,
Leaving the ghosts
Of solitude to rule.

It extinguishes
The fires of freedom
That burn, naturally,
In the hearts and minds
Of all.

Keep the Bantu of all nations
Everywhere
Drinking. The more
The merrier. The merrier
The better for the governments
Of apartheid everywhere
Who serve the death cups
To all who will drink,
Sleep, and never sound
The trumpets of love
The drums of oppression and
The chimes of freedom.

They will always win!
Unless we rise up
And refuse to drink
From their cups
That continue to disguise
Their victories
With our own vulnerabilities.

Son

for Shane

He comes peeking
His head through the clouds
To lay it upon
The soft shoulder of the horizon.

It is early
In his day.
It is early
In his life.

His imagination paints
Brush stroke after
Brush stroke upon
The canvas of his existence.

At times, he seems
Compelled to push
His determination and to force
His momentum.

At other times,
He sits quietly
Letting his mind wander
Into the mysticism of the fish bowl.

He wonders what
It would be like
To float endless
And to only hear
Murmurs from the world.

He feels he has done this
All before, somewhere before
He has poked his head
Through the clouds over
An uncertain horizon.

Hunting the Plebeian Sun

After scratching gravel from the ring,
After rubbing elbows with the sea,
After touching the twilight's hiss,
I cover shadows
Sleep by the wharf
And hunt through the labyrinth of skin.

It hurts to bargain skin for sun,
To toil labor for sin,
To barter wealth for movement,
But it pays well to trade
Laughter for poverty
Sweat for eyes
And touch for horizons
That are as smooth and as unruffled
As the new dawn.

Midwest

for Tyrone Williams

There's this dance
We do in the fields
Of the Midwest.
It's a cross
Between milking a cow
And fishing a smooth pond
That's the size
Of a small cosmetic mirror
Used for touching up
Before the *big* event.

There's this thing
We do in the Midwest
Called a dance. Up and down
The highways and the country roads,
Everyone calls it
By different names
But mostly we all know
It started at birth
In our bones—
A movement as unique
As corn in the field,
As the sweet in the tar
That holds the roads
Together connecting one
Farm to one neighborhood
And so on
And so on.
The wind whistling thru
The lawns of our hearts.

Desire

I want to
Peel my dreams
Like an onion
One thin layer
After the other
Paper thin—
Nothing between

I want to
Understand how
My heart moves
My dreams deep within
My chest beating and shaping
The divinity of life—
Solid and easy

I want to
Unlock this world free
Unknown desires
And patch it all
Together humble and clear

When She Looks Different

When she looks
Different at his
Face, there is
A certain pain visible
From deep in the darkness
Of her wandering soul
Which she hasn't honed
Since childhood.

The years dim
Become as stagnant as midnight
Boiling the ghosts
To life with steam.
Enchanted and devious
They roam her sleep
Waiting to strike her.
She wonders about the times
He took her out
To a dinner or a dance
And fed her well
And nursed her drunk
And took her love
Cashed it out
And left her broken,
Pulled by the roots.

When she looks
Different in his eyes
There is a hurt
Growing like a big, orange sun
From a very early horizon.
She knows how to suffer.
It's the only lesson
She has ever learned.

Open the Sky for Air

for Faruq Z. Bey

Crack it
Open. Widen the sky.
Let us stretch our necks
Through the hole created
To breathe in colors
That we can cultivate in our souls
And later make into words,
A love as bright as the stars
In the spectral night
Or rhythmical light.

Turn us on.
Make us believe
That color is a language
And that shadows can
Be brought to life
To dance us out
Of our solitude and darkness,
And into a world
Where the dawn is a metaphor
Written by the sun.

This Was the World

This was the world
Long before it began.
This was the plan:
A grandmother, somewhere, hanging
Laundry on a clothes line
In the springtime. A baby born
In the quiet of the wilderness
Of a dream just begun.

A baby born first
Grown to maturity later
Child to parent
Cycle continues.

But all that are
In this world were
Part of a history written
In the heart of a spirit
That seeded souls
Long before creation.

This was the plan,
And it happened.

Occasionally, I Lie Awake

Occasionally, I lie awake
In the universe of the sea.
I lie high upon a sandbar
Letting faint waves wash
Over and pass
Holding and releasing.

I think sometimes
It could all be different
And dry for me,
But there are other times
I believe
The only important thing
Is to have liquid
Wash through
The pores of myself.

I want it all.
I want it all badly.
The waves often feel
Like God whistling
A sweet harmony that glides
Over me and out
To the dark depths
Where legends are created
In the shadows of HIS music.

Last Will and Testament

for Cal

As if the end
Won't come
like a thief in the night.
As if the many we've loved
Won't ever leave us.
As if this dream
Could never be shattered.
As if we've never had trouble
Falling asleep to begin the dream.

Today
My heart is
As big as the world,
And all the people of all
The countries live inside
The walls of my chest.
They breathe and work,
And make me sing
An unfamiliar anthem of hope.

I will not be
Buried alone in the mud
Never to be heard from
Again. My heart will be
Heard loud and clear,
As the people inside me
Refuse to make changes
In the harmony of their love.
As if every one of them
Will remain forever silent.

I'm Not Writing Any Elegies

I'm not worried
Anymore about this
Or that or how
It will all end
Up. A friend,
A very good friend,
Once said that, "The time
Will be the time."

And that's for anything.
And that's for everyone.
"The time will be
The time." So I'm
Not writing any elegies about loss.
And I'll tell you this much,
The world is bigger
Than any poem.
And God is
Bigger than this world.

No, a good friend taught me
All about time.
I'm not worried.

The King Tree

We're playing it smart.
We've settled on the essentials:
An old baseball glove, or two,
An inexpensive Sears transistor radio,
A pocket full of dried weeds,
A rag ball and a razor blade.

We're playing for time
To rub up against the King Tree.
Time to build hope,
Time to remember all
Of the tears we let run
Down our cheeks
And into the dirt.

Yeah! We're playing it smart,
And we're settled.
We'll make this pact now.
Everyone cut your fingers.
We'll make this deal:
If we hold each other's
Dreams together, tight to our chests,
We'll never grow old,
And we'll never die.

First one to break
This deal ruins
The future
For us all.

Fishin'

I used to fish a lot.
I remember the smell
Of lake breezes swirling
Around inside of me
Like waves over my heart.
I felt serene.

Even now, when I get a chance,
I go to the shoreline,
Walk into the water
And transform myself
Into a bubble rising
Up in the dark, blue sky of the lake.
I rise to the top.
I am a star passing through
A galaxy of water.

Weightless—
I believe myself
To be an air bubble
Released from a fish
Floating on a trail
To the surface.

My Long, Long Driveway

One warm sunny day,
I sat on my front porch
Looking out over the lawn
Letting its smell
Rub up over my skin
Feeling as gentle
As an insect pulling sand
Through an afternoon shadow
Across my long, long driveway.

I remember the taste of weeds,
The smell of baseball hide,
And the flavor of freshly fallen rainwater.
I've always wanted to keep these things
Ready in the back of my dreams.

But it seems,
So many years later,
That recall will likely be slow,
And not anywhere as fast
As the coming of a new day.

I wonder now
If those summer days
Of baseball and playing in the fields
Will ever live again?
And if they do,
Will they mean as much
As an insect pulling a shadow
Over my skin
And across the rough cement
Of my long, long driveway.

A Bag of Catsup
for Cal

Here's the scene.
In the foreground,
There's a burst of color
As loud as life.
On the one hand I can
Hardly look at it,
Yet on the other, my eyes
Stick like glue.
I can't pull the life away
From my vision.
It is hung out
And lined up
Forever.

The reflection
Is a glowing prism.
It is like a spaceship
That I can remember seeing
In a cheap movie
While sitting in the darkened Shores Theater
With a big, brown bag full of french fries
Smothered in catsup,
Leaking through the bag
Staining my pant leg.

I have since thought about that brown bag.
If I had it now,
To hold in my hands,
I would neatly fold it,
Like a flower,
And press it into a Bible.

I don't have that bag,
And I don't have a Bible,
But I believe I still have that spirit.
I believe I caught it
In a dream.

Recently
I can remember caressing the feeling,
And pressing it
Into the pages of my thoughts.
I pushed it hard
And deep.

But someday,
Like a burst of life,
I know it will rush
Hot
Through my veins,
And it'll show itself
Right then and there!
You just wait and see!
Maybe I'll scrape my knee on cement somewhere?
Maybe I'll cut my finger with a fish hook?
Or maybe I'll take a bullet in my heel?
But you just wait and see
If as soon as the air hits my blood,
If it don't turn into a bag of catsup,
In a theater,
In a small town,
And like a flickering image on a screen,
I will disappear
Leaving the smell of grease
And a small burst of life
To settle, like a worn cloud,
Into the fabric of a ragged, old theater chair.

Blood in the Moon

Under a cucumber moon,
Oblong in my dreams,
Notions from the underbrush
Pump blue in my heart.

Sassy talk from clovers,
Whispered at times,
Runs naked through the mud
And climbs cool in my blood.

An unknown rhythm,
Talks of leaves,
That shade eyelids
From the dancing night.

Pound and pump.
Pump and pound.
Veins across the moon
Stretched out
Like rusted fence
And suffered in the rain dirt
To poke holes through
The hearts of the earthworms.

Pound and pump.
Pump and pound.
Blues in the brush
Oblong in the clover
Sassy is my cool blood
Naked
Unknown
Shade across the veins
Eyelids dance
In the night time leaves
In the full-phase of dreams.

Imagine

for Jeff

What if
I could
Retrace every step
Down every path I've walked?

What if
I could
Go back to that old neighborhood,
Salute every old friend
Like the first days
Of our beginnings?

What if
Standing there behind
The rain of my memory
Was my old, old pal,
Blond and blue,
Waiting and waiting and waiting
For me to bring
The news of the future
Back to the past?

What if
Everyday measured and equaled
A lifetime shaped, never bent,
With happiness and light?

What if
All this history
Was not our own?

What if
I had never been
A young boy alone
But forever alive?

What if
We could retrace every step
To follow ourselves back home
To the souls of our creation?

Mother's Day

The last time
I saw my mother
Alive she danced
Herself out of the rain
Of her broken heart.

Alive she danced
More than I
Had ever seen her.
Across the daybreak
And into the sunset.
She was happy.

For once, Gershwin didn't stop.
The music played
Until every last note was laced
Into the fibers
Of her dark, blue soul.

I thought
It only worked this way
In film or on stage,
But on Mother's Day
I learned
That standards can be broken
As easy as a heart.

And My Father Died

My father
Turned away from me
And pulled tubes
From a respirator and other
Hospital machines into
The growing darkness of his soul.
The night had come.
And it was slipping away
Fast into the twilight of his spirit.
He called my name out.
About 2:30 a.m. I saw
The letters in my name float
Out in a mist
From his purple colored chest.

This all happened
In a sterile room,
In a sterile building
Where death often hides
Like the thin hair
Of cobwebs spun
In the corners of the night.

Again, I saw a faint mist rise
Above my father's head,
And, again, my name focused
In a spray near the ceiling
Of the sterile room.
He spoke,
With a weak voice,
About dreaming the night before.
In his dream he saw us
Together like the branches of a tree.
He saw all of his life
And he recalled all of the details:
Carrying me to bed
After falling asleep
In his strong arms—

Talking to me
The night before kindergarten was to start—
Every bit of every vacation
Spent in Upper Michigan—
And the many inside jokes
That held our family together
Tight!

But, by 3:00 a.m.,
All had quieted
And the mist of my name
Was gone. And
His soul has escaped
Into the blackness of the night.

The Dog Died Too

The dog died.
I grieved for a long time
One Saturday afternoon.
The world looked like
A gray cyclone fence
Surrounding a dog,
At its center—
A dead dog,
How can this world afford
To take time out
To notice a dog,
In its casket—
On its side—
Rigor mortis set
Deep into animal's body
And owner's soul?
My goddamn dog!
It was more than that.
A lot more than that.

The Train Is Your Blood

The train is your blood
Pulling everything up
By the roots as you shine
One last time
Like a coin being tossed
Deep into a blue fountain.

Somewhere you may rust
Waiting to change the world
That doesn't accept movement
Because it knows so little
About standing still.

I Used to Live in a Home

for Jack Driscoll

When I left
The house, I packed up
All my things
And I took a piece
Of the cobwebs from the corner
And rubbed it into
My sweaty, sad face
And I dragged some
Across my dying soul.
I hoped
A small part of me
Would come back
To life. I thought
The webs could act
As smelling salts and keep
Me from slipping
Deeper and deeper
Into the tiles
Of myself.

I almost evaporated
When the time came
To leave that old place.
I turned to look
One last time:
Three bedrooms,
A small bathroom
With cracked, mildew ceiling,
A living room's sleepy fireplace
That had been the witness
To the happiness and heartaches
Of cold Christmas Eves and damp Easter mornings.

I left
My image in the gray
Smoked bathroom mirror.
Pulling the plug

On my past,
I floated out
To the street
Like rain water.
I was free
Outside, but part of me
Remains, still, inside
In the mirror,
On the wall,
In the bathroom
Of that old house.

Ale So Pale

Bubbly, foamy, rising
Luck.
Champagne color of liquid.
It spurts and squirts
All high tonight.

Soothing, grieving
Hungry head.
Hold down,
The sound,
Of crashing , swirling night lights
Dimmed slower and slower and
Slower—slight.

Coming from the Sea

Coming from the sea,
My luggage packed,
Neatly sorted,
I pulled even
With a shoreline
Etched in a clay
Made from the bones
Of human skulls.

I raised my head
High above the rocks
To level and balance the black
Sky with the blue sea.
Stars rolled from my hair
And broke into seashells
Just three, no more than five,
Inches below the surface of the water.

I've come up
From the deep
To be with you
In this world of clay and bone.
I've come to sleep
At the base of your skull,
Just below
The waves of your dreams
That toss you awake
Each night.

Dark Spirit

I walked.
For the first time,
In many months,
I walked the streets.
I did not feel
Great as I dragged myself
Along scraping and gouging
Bloodlines into my
Shallow, pale soul,
Where I have hidden
For quite some time now.

I don't know!
I feel like everything
I never wanted to be.
I feel like chalk
Being scraped into cement.
I feel like a nightstick
Hitting a striker's teeth.
I feel my own
presence haunts me.

I wanted to walk today.
Alone.
That's all I wanted to do.
But somehow I ended up
Feeling like a dark spirit
As weightless fog.
Yet as heavy as a heart.

After the Boxes
There's Still a Neighborhood

for Dennis Chabot

After the boxes
Are filled and closed,
And after the grass
Is cut one last time,
And after you've smeared
Your tears and sweat
All over your face and beard,
There will still be
A neighborhood standing
Close to a shoreline
Heaped with the smells
Of fried dinners and boyhood romp.

Someday they'll decide
To close the whole thing
Up and carry it away
Like a standard size suitcase.
But that won't be anytime
Soon. You won't have to worry
When that will happen
Because you've built a future
On much less before.

No, someday yes,
They'll close the boxes
And cut the grass
And smear your boyhood memories
Up and down the shoreline
Of that old neighborhood.

Deliver Me

(Christian Poems)

Holy Saturday

Jesus is Waiting
—Al Green

This is my poem to the world
On the eve of resurrection.
Alone, I have twisted
My soul into unrecognizable shapes
Neoned by negative spirits
Circled like killing fields
Of introspective sorrow.

This is my poem to a world
That is too busy talking—too
Busy with its fighting to
Stop from hurting
Each other. And that's alright
Because in the end, no poem,
No poet, no speech,
No speaker, no politician
No person: mother, father
Brother or sister will matter
At all. It will come down to this—
Either all knees will bend and
All tongues will confess that Jesus Christ is Lord,
Or they won't!

But while I breathe my poem into this world
And beyond, I will bend my knees
And confess all
My sins before Jesus
Christ, creator of all my poems,
On this eve of eternity and forgiveness.

I Have Been Washed

for W. H. Auden

I have been washed
In the rich, saving blood
Of Jesus my Lord.

The bread and the wine,
Spiritual detail spent
To comfort my mind.

The unsoothed, jeopardized life
The devil's beckoning power lent
To create a world broken

With terror and strife. There will be
Many attempts to put life
In some significant perspective,

But the most any of us can do,
Alone, is temporal healing. No resurrecting
Feeling, low buried deep beyond

What is
Important to an everlasting
Life. I have been washed in

The living blood
Of Jesus Christ the Lord.

Deliver Me

I have broken
Voodoos like vows promised
Before the Lord. All
Has come to nothing for me
Waiting alone for the sun,
Unknown in most corners,
But truly known in God's circle
Present everywhere at all times. God,
Please deliver me!

I have asked many
Questions to find
No answers. There is only one
Source to find the one
Answer I need, and all
Humankind can use, everywhere
At all times. God,
Please deliver me!

Rivers rise with empty desire,
Which forever remains
Broken twigs in God's plan.
Desire is not achievement. It comes
As easy as any wave, white capped
And broken against the shore. The river
Runs endless, leaving me
To chant, pray and break
Voodoos of my own desires.
God, please deliver me
From evil,
For thine is
The kingdom and the glory
Forever and ever—Amen.

Symphony of the Flesh

This is my symphony of the flesh
rising, balancing high to reach
My Lord, unmatched beyond any
One's imagination. Love unbound
And released to feed all
Who hunger. Quench all
Who thirst. Soothe all
Who burn in pain
From fire, earthbound in torturous
Rein. The devil's plan is masterful,
But it cannot equal the Master's.
O Lord teach me what you have
Known from the beginning,
"Forgive them, and they are
Forgiven." And so all must be
Included in my symphony
Of flesh, offered before the rapture,
When in the night You come
To take your faithful home
To peace and holy eternity.

Woodstock Morning

As this new day unfolds
To envelop with sunshine all
That rises from sweet, sweet earth
Below, the resurrected sun
Brings forth breath for the small lungs
Of mountain flowers grown
Amongst broken yellowed leaves,
Treasures left by autumn past
And winter's only memories of life
And death, mixing down lo
Into the valleys, bearing witness
To deer, possum, twig, and Christ.
This new day is a mirror
To all who will
Come alive
Forever.

Living in the Material World

I have fallen before
Through the clouds of the lonesome
Earth's soul, darkened and bruised
Oceans of discontent flooding
Shorelines, inward, retracting the dawn
From every edge of night.

People stumble
Upon each other's misfortunes,
Waiting long into the twilight of destruction
And death. No life nowhere
And there's more of the same
In the evenings of our original sins.

People may believe
They can master all
Things, complete every task, but the world
Breaks just a little everyday at first
And later it will fall
Wide open. Difficult year after
Difficult year will build tomorrows
Unimagined, relentless in evil.

Some may ignore themselves now,
But others will plead
Forgiveness from God,
While many will eventually spread
Themselves into low, flatness like ashen
Bones to settle across the country
Of disconnected spirits. From God
many will fall, with much
Wailing and gnashing of teeth,
To an eager material world
Whose arms will open wide
With much empty nothingness,
More eternal angst,
And unholy, hopeless promises.

Roll Away the Stone

Today I walked free
Out of the dark tomb of myself.
Resurrected and thoroughly connected
Back to the Holy Spirit of life.

All of my years amassed
Like crows on rows and rows
Of telephone wires filling the lonely
Fields in the America of my nights.

Alone, too long, I've tasted
Darkness; my feast to the emptiness
of my hollow, pale soul that once was
Shallow and forbidden—prayerless and uneasy.

Today I claim victory over
The death of this world
Greater love I've not known
Than One Lord—One Faith—One Baptism.

The Anti-War Politics of Christ

In the garden, He made it
All so simple, "He who lives
By the sword shall die
By the sword." And he
Healed His enemy's
Wounded ear.

Stripping the Adult Century Bare

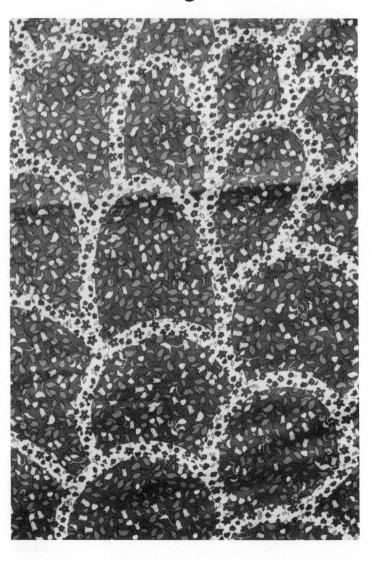

Cats of My Youth

I remember the calico cats of my youth,
Youthful tapestry of color and wit
Lying beneath the long tables of my dreams
Wanting only to recall the past.

I remember angry trees shaking,
Connecting with the trembling sky,
Steadying the earth's lonely
memory of itself.

I remember my early years as fresh
Scents lingering in the mornings of my
Future. Those bending days
That grew old inside themselves.

I remember I once had dreams
As tight as little fists
Knotted with inspiration
In the heart of my youth.

I, still, remember what
those calico cats of
my past meant.

Harry Carey Said So

Did you say your prayers?
Did you kiss your mom today?
Did you put only mustard on your hotdog?
Did you ever think about baseball?

Baseball,
Some even say holy, holy baseball.
A game spread
Out on a field
With infinity as dimensions
And folks saying things like
"Racin' to the bag."
"High Hard One."
And "maybe—maybe
Outta here."
Did you say your prayers?

Baseball,
All the ambitions
benched, riding the lonesome pine,
Or first string, riding the top.
Majors and minors.
The very life of man
Made longer by men
Touching corners
And circling diamonds.
Did you kiss your mom today?

Baseball,
"Goin back . . . goin back . . .
And he makes the catch!"
Say holy—holy!
See the bleachers filled with life?
That's happy, happy life
Moving and swaying together
Under the sun and moon
Screaming from the back:
"Hit the ball!"
"Would ya hit the ball ya jerk?"

It's happy.
It's holy.
Did you put only mustard on your dog?

Baseball,
Extra innings all the way.
Action to stop the world.
To break the records
To fill your space
and it's holy.
Holy—Holy Cow
And Harry's healed
And he's come home to breathe
Life from up there
Right up there, behind home plate.
That's where he fills the pictures
With words from our youth
Oh Harry—it's holy!
Did you ever think about baseball?

Fats

For Scharaazetta

He was a cherub,
Somebody else's angel boy,
Wide impish grin,
Square hair and rhythm
Beyond his time. Seldom lamenting
Thrills from the hill
That Elvis stole—took and turned
Into an ice cream sundae
Song without color—faded
Out blues. Beyond
Hill after hill sits the real
King. Livin' large. Voice
Like royalty. His pain hidden
Behind a smile (nothin
New) showing itself rarely.
For this king, it's only Rock'N'Roll
Through a universe of so many
Twinkling keys.

Assassination

My father, who had
Worked hard all his life, sat
Across the table
From me and my mother
With his big, calloused hands folded,
Bruised and red
Like a small pile of house bricks.
His dreams were made from honest work.

My father, who had
Worked hard all his life, sat
Up late on the night
Of the 1960 elections.
He told me about hope
And prosperity for working
People under democratic
Leadership. In this world
We have the freedom to work
And earn. He told me of good
Times to come. I could tell,
From across the table, by the upward
Turn of his smile
He was happy. That morning
From the east, a new sun
Warm and rising
Like his own occasional joy.

Since then, it has all come
And gone like a whisper,
My father and his dreams.

When the World Was a Flower

for Pamela

When the world was a flower,
When the horizon was a ritual
Of new blood rising in the veins
Of our new love,
When hope was as present
As happiness before Eden . . .
I want to go back
To those times
When we fed our future on a wish
Riding it all
Staying out late
Wondering about what
It would be like
To worry a lifetime
And to commit ourselves.
Souls deep down.
Connected spirits.
This was us.
Just as we had planned it down
To the wild life we created with
Words as simple as the sun
Shining as in our first summer.
Flowers and ritual horizons.

Love, like a prophet,
Found us lost
Inside the purple darkness of ourselves
And brought us up
        To be
           together.

II. Apocalypse Now!

No, they did not bury me, though there is a period of time which I remember mistily, with a shuddering wonder, like a passage through some inconceivable world that had no hope in it and no desire.
—from *Heart of Darkness,* Joseph Conrad

Just because some of us can read and write and do a little math, that doesn't mean we deserve to conquer the universe.
—from *Hocus Pocus,* Kurt Vonnegut, Jr.

Woodstock Nation

Our generation got soul!
—Jefferson Airplane, 1968

Nope!
They're never gonna believe
This some 10-20-30
Or more years from now.

Nope!
They're never gonna believe
That a half-million young people
Sat around on a big, ole hog farm
In the middle of nowhere
For an entire weekend
Making love, talking peace, and listening
Hour after hour
To ubiquitous rock'n'roll.

This shit ain't never gonna flush
10-20-30 or more
Years from now
With the *Less than Zero* Generation,

In the future,
It will be hard for young people
To believe in a world

Where Love was an anthem
Played in a farmer's field
Away from the cities
And deep in the soul.

Drugs

My face is pressed
Against a damp, gray sky.
My spirit melts
Quickly down a window pane
And into the floor.

I am crabby
As I try to force
My world into
A light beam
From a very close star.

I think I'm depressed.
I think about biting
My own teeth.
My spine rolls up and down
Like a worn, yellowed window shade.
I know I've had this feeling before,
And I don't remember liking it.
But then, again, I'm not sure!
I don't think I like
A symphony playing high
Volume in my highway head.
Just at this moment I turn
My head into a busy street.
I see cars float past
In fragmented parts.
I see white pavement lines
Like hyphens
In my dreams.
I am terrified,
So I bark.
My noise spells words
Across the crimson sky:
"Red sky in morning
 Sailors take warning—
"Red sky at night
 Sailors delight."

My mother says these words
From her anxious grave.
I see her words rise from the dirt
And evaporate through the pores
In my skin and into the fibers
Of the millions of muscles and nerves
In my body.
I ache!
My eyes want to run out
Of their sockets and into my mouth
I wonder how I let myself
Get this way.
I let the symphony play
While tires and tailgates from broken autos
Float, heaven-like, past me.
I turn to myself
And say: "I can take the visual hallucinations,
But I can't stand the audio ones!"
I'm on a street again,
Walking faster than my shoes.
I step on a spider.
It screams!
I scream!
And I sweat.
I sweat so much that I feel water
Dripping out of my half-dollar size pupils.
I am taking in too much light.
I bend into a candle
To light my cigarette.
Some wax sticks to the end.
I puff hard,
But get no smoke.
I laugh,
And call it a "bummer cigarette."
I next decide to climb
Into the test pattern on the color TV.
I cross the channels
To get deeper
Into the picture.
I run past a commercial
In progress and onto another street.

I look up at the sky.
It is still gray.
I decide to stay put
On the street
Until morning
Or until the music stops.

Stick This Up!

So time has come
And time has passed
And some have said
That we "are
Closer to nowhere"
And others have said,
"let bygones be bygones"
And I say,
"I can forgive
But I cannot forget"
My life as a struggle
Meant too much to me
My dreams hurt
And broken too much
To me it was
Like pouring a fever
Into my heart
(A very, very young heart)
Tortured and broken in 1968
King-Kennedy-Chicago-Vietnam
Like Zapruder's film before
And Cronkite's war after
Pulling images close
Into my brain
I thought it a volcano
Erupting leaving me
For dead on the beach
Of my stripped soul
Crying out for GOD
And being sent the KKK, John Birchers, and
Fundamentalist preachers resurrecting
The Old South as a new religion
While the other cultures drank
Themselves sick
Losing children in the night
In the jungles
Through the years

In this America
of their sleep and now
I say I can
Forgive but I can't forget
Lining up my brothers and sisters
In Ohio like ducks
Popping them off
While they played
Their rock'n'roll
Begging them to join
The side of the right
And to leave behind
The left—new and idealistic
And now with the neighbor boy
Dead and gone
A man turns to me
And says, "Remember, back during the war?"
Confused and scarred
I reach out
For all the names of the dead
That have written my book
That have left this record
Entrusted to stone
Settled like rust
At the bottom of our hearts
These names are serious business
And every one I press
To my heart warming
Each beat from the cruel
Cold marble tomb
That wears each year hence
In the night I scream
Out I can forgive
But we must
Never forget

Decoration Day

for Dennis Manning

A couple of days after
The news reached the States,
His mother's heart broke
Never to mend itself.
With his last breaths,
he took his family and friends
Hostage into the darkness
Of the world's sin.

There's no turning back
The clocks. They cannot be
Adjusted to read the present
Time, when the future has died, alone
Somewhere, in another place.

And the newspapers will write
About it and the TV will
Talk about it, but no one
Will ever tell this story
The way it really happened.
The way it was supposed
To have happened in a town,
In a life somewhere, unknown.

And this business of murder
Bruises each rising sun
Above every American town.
Towns that were never
More than small dots
On small maps, routing death
To innocent lives that
Will be forever lost
In the rapid fire
Of the jungle night.

Because everyone can't
Believe it,

Doesn't mean it didn't
Happen!

Because everyone didn't
See it,
Doesn't make it
untrue!

Because everyone
Hurts,
Doesn't make it Stop!

Because after twenty years
They'll have forgotten your names
Doesn't mean you never
Existed!

Because you did live,
Doesn't mean
You'll remain
A memory!

Because it is,
It is!

And you can't reappear
For the benefit of the few
Who doubted all along.
Injustice is the law here
Dear boy. Here where
You grew up where
You dreamed, not where
You died. Not where
They took you,
Laid you out,
Neatly uniformed,
Placed you in the funeral
Home of the Far East.
The whole thing planned,
Planned to the smallest detail,
Except for your mother's broken heart.

The Surface of Murder

for Jeff, Allison, Sandy and Bill
With Much Love

The world can never be
the same after you
have backed into a ghost.
A spirit trapped just
below the surface of murder.

Someday some people will tell
you it never happened,
at least not the way
it was said to have
happened. Death alone.

No place to lie down
and rest itself. Death
That can break your heart
and take with it every
body's dreams and memories.

Cold rain never felt
this lonely, this dark
And ghosts have never ever
been this close to us,
for if they had, we would

have realized this history
coming long before
we were ever created,
souls seeded with spirits becoming
human, returning back to dust
to be sprinkled just below
the surface of murder.

And I Ain't Never Gonna See
Bobby Rush No More!

It's all patchwork.
It's memory as a photograph here
And there. It adds up
To be your masterpiece,
Paint as thick
As your own heartbeat.

These days you can wish
Upon a star if you want,
But that ain't gonna change
Anything. You are still
Going to have
Autumns as gray as your dreams.
Cold, wet winters. It never
Ends, never turns around. The future
Can't be backed out of. It's straight
Ahead or nothing.

And you can fret it, realize
It, or not. Go tell it
On some mountain if you want,
But you ain't never gonna see
The pathways of your youth
Again. Not in this life
Time. Not in this world
That spends its time grazing
Upon galaxies feeding upon stars.

All any of us will get
Is farther from ourselves.

We'll just keep losing
Little pieces of our pasts,
Just like Bobby Rush, or any other
Old Childhood
Friend first, and all
The rest after.

Ride Your Youth Bareback

for Jim Gustafson

As if some people really have
A choice to ride or not
To ride their youths bareback
Like wild horses out
On the western plains, twisted
And rolled land, like tough scars
Born from gashes cut
From birth.

As if anyone can close the hurt
That fills open sores
Like broken windows stopping
The cold, darkness of midnight
Pain, catching sideways behind the bones
Of the soul.
This is not a setback!

So many want to say
That poetry is not
Truth, but simply art,
And you, Jim, sweet bard reply,
"But I gotta tell you Honey,
Don't let it break your heart,
But there ain't no money, Honey!
No Money in Art!"
Yet, from the light between
Earth and dark, mud of grave,
William Carlos Williams whispers
To us all that "Men die
miserably every day
for lack
of what is found there."
So we ride it bare
Back cause it's the only truth
We know.
We ride it.

Paper Ghost Rain Dance

You know, I can
Often see rice paper ghosts
Dancing in the eyes of young men
Whose lives seem to swing
Like dim lightbulbs
High in old farmhouse bedrooms,
Lonely movement on very thin wire.

And no one ever sees
The sameness of change
Occurring just as if
It never happened.

I say, what's the difference
If you die now
or later? Who's gonna weep
If they put you down
Deep into the ground next
To some or other young soldier
Or, perhaps, shoulder to shoulder
With the devil himself.

These are the chances
You take when you pull
A trigger, trip a land mine,
Shoot to kill, or fire
When you see the whites
Of their eyes

I'm afraid
I'll forever see
Rice paper ghosts dancing
With death in the windows
Of very young skulls,
As music plays off
Bleached white bones
Like the heavy rains
of Vietnam.

Deep Down Darkness Lasts Forever

I heard them say
That deep down darkness lasts
Forever in the flash
Of a lighted flame burning
Amber, glowing, as white as a ghost's
Hot blood flowing thin in its midnight
Veins—transparent. I heard
Them say that far away is really closer
To a melancholia grin than to a nightmare rage
Burning beyond. The Proverbs speak
Testaments of battles that take the night
Time's lives further into eternity.
I heard them say
That whispers can destroy more
Than simple talk can repair.
I heard.
I heard them say more
Than they could
Ever imagine.

Rising, Like the Bottom

for Steven Schreiner

through the window,
I watched a morning
rising, slowly, like the bottom
of a smooth, crystal glass

from around the edges,
I stared at a leaning
ladder, lonely against
a tree, crooked to the world
yet more straight than any
sun, balancing
upon any horizon.

sky as blue as midnight
in so many ways brighter
than snow. On a morning
like this, doves charm only
themselves. A crooked ladder leaning
against a tree makes much
sense out of beauty.

The Lazarus Dream Forgiven

for Todd Duncan

I have and you have.
We all have had
Our Lazarus dream
Before. Somewhere we've reached
Out like ghosts
With hands as faint and pale
As still water lying
Along the banks of closed
Streams. We have wondered
About children like us
That remain buried
Within the skin of our own
Weak desires. We never get
Used to the pain that soaks us
Thick like rags, stopping
Dams, holding back
The currents of our futures. Slowly
We want to float, or have
Someone like us float, out
Of ourselves, just like Lazarus
In the darkness of the cave,
As lonely as his once distant soul,
Before the living waters
Nurtured him back
To life. One piece. All
Forgiven.

Morrissey

I'm going to
Cut of all my
Hair on just one side
Of my head and puff
Up the other side real high
Lookin' like a cross between
Elvis, in *G. I. Blues*, and Freddie
Flintstone on TV. Next, I
Too am going to
Put so many earrings in one
Of my two ears, so
I look like John Wayne's cowboy boots
In *Rooster Cogburn*. Cool
As all this were, I, too,
Am going to sing some
Moaning songs about pissing
On the future of post-
Modern fate. Disguise myself
As a new beginning. Call it Cyber
Spaced out-junk-bonded
Puked up, Scooby-Dooed,
Surrealistic, Plastic Pillow of
Sleeping dogs lying endless Black
Out. I want lots of black stuff:
Black pants, black shirts, black socks
And, especially, black boots with
Little silver chains
That jingle-jangle-jingle. Cool.
So you know that I don't belong
To any sub-group, super group:
Political. Social. Philosophical or
Otherwise. I'm just making
Money, lots of it.
Money! Moaning
"Viva Hate" and
Up your nose
With a rubber hose.

Censored

When it comes to the secret
Of our afternoons spent, all
Too often, we think we know
Or at least thought we knew, each other's
Dilemmas, but time after time, the fact
Remains that we have always been
Too busy searching to find
What has always been there.
We are afraid. It is that plain
And simple. We dread the fact
That someone else may discover
Our loneliness and our fear.
The medicine man shakes
His fiery torch and his bag of miracles,
And we begin to nervously think
Of ways to mask what we may feel
In our hearts. The truth
brings trouble to our sleep
And into our safe dreams. It brings down
Our past into rivers at our feet.
And we tremble that, perhaps, someone,
Somewhere knows something more than we
Will ever realize. It is our own darkness
That haunts our hearts. It is not
The idea that we may learn
Too much to inflict harm upon our intellects,
Or that we may challenge ourselves
Into the depths of all reason—
In this life and beyond. Somewhere
We learned that it is not healthy to dream
And to know, or even think for,
Ourselves. We tremble
And turn from
This point on.

Watching Charles Bukowski Look-a-Like w/Autistic Boy in Old Chevy w/Bubblegum Patches on Worn Tires Makes Me Think . . .

I hate Republicans!
They never look like Bukowski.
And they are less likely to be
Autistic. They have fewer
Cases of birth defects.

They have it all:
Money, education, and health
Care. All Republicans have
A genuine, real deal, health plan,
And their plans don't include
The rest of us whose mothers and fathers slaved
Over oil dripping, rivet belching
machines and over ovens
In hot, hot kitchens.

And they always have new tires
on brand new cars. Those bastards
Are free spirits because we
Lighten their loads.
Our sweat soaked souls labor
Much for little
Time to spend with our own

Families. Valuable as time is,
We have not
The leisure to forget
About punching a clock—
Breaking for lunch—
Or even killing a little time!
Hell!! We'd like to *kill*
A little time, before it kills us.
But those Republicans always seem
To come up with this day

Light savings legislation.
So we keep losing
Hours. For us it is
Really spring forward, fall back, fall
Back and you're laid
Off. And that's where
These Bukowski look-a-likes w/autistic boys
Fit in. Why is it
That lonely, old men
And young boys should have
To drive around in old, beat-up Chevys,
With worn, old tires and litter
Filled backseats: mail addressed
To "Occupant" and Nintendo game codes
Scribbled here and there?

Why is it that children should
Have to sit in backseats moving back
And forth, merging seizure
With hot, fast food dinner
Burning their lips between
Neighborhoods, street lights, stop
Signs and plenty
Of yields? While Republicans seem
To get the "real" God, new
Cars, even expensive fast
Foods. While the rest get lost
And found and lost
Again between heartbreaks and elections,
A very systematic devaluation. I saw
A sign recently—it read
"Abortion the American Holocaust," and
I thought, "Hey!
Republicans the new Holocaust!"
Those genocidal, fake, fat ass sneaks
Deserve nothing more than they give
To Bukowski look-a-likes
w/autistic boys
In old Chevys
With bubblegum patches
On worn, old, recapped tires.

Conservative Song

The music of conservative nerves
Rattles through their thin veins
Hidden within their own bruised purgatory,
Tortured beneath their skin.
Unparalleled in (his)
Story. Revelation strikes
Still the midnight notions
Of the blackbird musical staffs aligned
To create a minor score that diminishes
Each note as quickly as the wind can
Move the proverbial one flailing hand
That beats upon itself to recreate
The audience's appreciation
For their ruptured dreams and displaced
movement. A nightmare is their calling card.

The conservative mind is the stifling
Puke vector of non-motion
And the abeyant healing of the lonely
Hearted. Where hope can be a soothing
Meditation to strengthen the dark
Muscles of our tense moonlights,
The radiant nights stars cut
Across our country highlighting the
Displaced, disinherited locations where the conservative
Song refuses to be sung. Conservative good moves slow
Through their blind, hardened hearts. So slow
that it does not recognize the spilled red blood—
O Palestine cries, O Hanoi cries, O Baghdad cries,
O Panama cries, O Grenada cries—and
Continues to cry throughout the horror being
Reigned upon their deserts and jungles
By the seemingly cosmic conservative
Control. Non-progressive, neo-conservative,
Post bardic babblers lacing the night, extinguishing
All hope by sweetening,
Perhaps, the music of the oppressed.

117

The harmony of the conservative song
Is a symphony to be raked under
The skin of the many
Temples of seductive silence.

Time Against the Wall

I.

There were once small stones.
I kept them private,
Always hidden away. They were
My personal mementos of the suffering
World. The tortured years
That fell, slowly, like stage curtains
On my innocence. I thought,
Perhaps, that I deserved something
Other than dark, secret lies. Thousands
Dead. Teenagers popped
Open like ripe sunflower seeds
Populating underground neighborhoods
Growing beneath the sidewalks' cracks, spreading
Like black-brown tombstones marking graves
Like weeds—stepped on—side
stepped—My trail is not unique,
But it has, in the end, led me
Home to clouds I have
Found just above my shoulders,
Surrounding the grayness of my soul.

II.

One early, cold December
Day, I saw a thousand burning
Huts across a small suburban lake.
My lake, I thought, protected forever.
I didn't think I would ever have to surrender
Its shores. I thought the wasted washed up sea
Shells were just smaller parts
Of its existence. Their exhausted presence
Came as an omen from a distant sun.

Through the moon's shadows, I rose
And became a witness to the many
Entrapped midnight souls who had been
Murdered in the waters of my own
Personal, dark, earth lake.
My country.
Human?
Humane?
I can now smell the loss.
Many lives have been buried deep
In the measured mud. The raging
Soil raptures the young back
From their own dismissed history
To live in an eternity that can not be
Split open like over-ripened seeds.
Spat out. Dark seeds growing
Into bad spirits, moving
Under yesterday's sidewalks.

III.

Not too long ago I
Reached for the spiritual hand of my ghost
Self, and I packed it all up
And headed away from my old neighborhood.
The abandoned seashell that I had become
Decided to head East,
Decided to resolve the national nightmare
I could not forget. I tried to vanish
The sight of the final smile, below
The neighbor boy's sad, young eyes.
My heart became a trigger of despair.
Dismissing youth,
Torturing trust,
Dragging secret, dark dreams
Into the mystic, black hole
Of America. I wanted to follow
A path that might lead
Through the gates of glory and freedom.

The national prayer that a young boy's death was
Supposed to answer. No handsome memories.
I could not find glory or freedom
Or hope or America.
Out there, beyond the burning
Suburban lakes, beyond the thousands
Of premature deaths, I found only
The horror—the horror—
The civil war
Of bone-leg-arm-mind and
blessed, holy souls. I could no longer follow
The long, shadowed road seeded
With many young spirits who would never
Be able to leave
Their tombstones of *our* past.
However, now, I feel they do remain
Alive just to forgive *us*
Our trespasses
As we did not theirs.

IV.

And so, after the many mean decades,
It is time to bid thee farewell
Sweet, sweet, innocent neighbor
Boy. They left you in a mud field
Of another country—alone, nowhere close
To our once blue, suburban lake,
but now it is more than time for me
To entrust your young soul to the multitude
Of stars. Drift to wherever your spirit will
Remain eternal. And while I will not hear
Your boyish laughter again, I will never forget
You as a young child who loved
The world so much that he gave
His own life to save us.
From what we all would soon become

It has been a long road now,
And an even longer wall to walk.
I see my blurred, fragmented reflection between
Each letter of every engraved name.
You will always live here and beyond!
A fellow soldier has brought me here
To see you one final time,
And he has allowed me the time
To weep and to begin to heal—time
That was never allowed to you.
Finally, I have realized
That your life was not about death;
It was really about love.
No greater love has he
Who will lay his own life down
For another. When I return
Back to my home, by the shoreline
Of our blue suburban lake,
I will pray for your life
For teaching me so much about America—
And even more about myself.

The Dream of Life I Once Was

"Goodbye drunken ghost."
—Allen Ginsberg's final words to Jack Kerouac

One Ohio morning, I awoke
To dream a life
That had its murky beginnings
Long before I was born.

Distant, far beyond what I could
Fully recall, were old
Friends. Friendships I had
Nurtured like small lambs
With the milk of my childhood.

Somehow my dream, my life,
Moved and exploded into thousands
Of different philosophies, directions and ideas.
Somehow, I became
Tangled in the webs of my memories
And I lost the grip on my old friends'
Hands. Friendships I had force
Weaned, but I did more. I did
Worse. I forgot
Them. I left
Them. I never returned
Until I was too far out
Beyond, and it was too late to return
To those days of innocent
Child's play. But I have
Grown just enough
To hear the bellowing
From my ghost-friends' whispers,
Their very faint voices tell
Me to put my ear against
The giant seashell of any neighbor's backyard
And to listen to the sea of myself
Rolling and wailing. Their voices,
In and Out, moving and pumping
The aging blood in my heart.

John Lennon Comes Back to New York City to Pay Homage to Bob Dylan

He comes back
A little pale, but no worse
For the wear and tear of being
Away, in another dimension,
For some twelve odd years. Now,
He knows everything
Is off the record. Things have changed
A lot and a little since he left
In early December 1980.
But he doesn't think in those terms
Anymore. Where he's been there is
No time, no dates to remember, no
Appointments to keep, no
Memory of a past or a present
At all. He pauses, for what to some might seem
A minute or two, on a city corner. He thinks
To himself that *he hasn't thought*
To himself in a long, long time,
And he knows there is now no concern
About measurements. No dates—no time—no years.
These things used to cause him pain. The future
Is always happening for him.
So, once again, he finds himself
In New York City, beloved home
Away from home. City
Where he has always felt
Comfortable and safe. If a person could see
Him now and approach him, gently,
And if that person were to suggest murder,
He wouldn't understand, nor would he
Consider the idea. He would swiftly dismiss
It, as quickly as waving away the vague
Street clouds rising from city grids.
Lennon glances up to see
A sign, lights flashing
Through a crowd. He recognizes

A building. He thinks he has been
There before. He sees, but he can't
Be seen. He likes that. It fits
His style—both, then and now. He checks
Around for a street name to remember
Where he might be. He believes
He knows where he is.
He smiles. He overhears people
Talking about Bob Dylan, and something
Seems to be going on here, but he "Doesn't know
What it is." He chuckles to himself. He is
The thin man. Everyone has come
To pay homage, to sing songs,
To celebrate old friends, and he too
Wants to pay his respect because he and Bob
Go way back to England days. Before Dylan
Was as he later became. Before electric
Guitar mania at Newport, before motorcycle nightmares,
Before guru love, before Berkeley in the 60's, before
There ever was a Sgt. Pepper. Before . . . He thinks
About a young Bobby Zimmerman riding
In the back of a rented Bentley, joking
Through the streets of London, a mighty long way
From Hibbing and Duluth. Dylan poking
Fun at American folk-a-rockers, et al.
Lennon is stoned, and Dylan, too, is way gone,
With a small movie camera running, capturing them
And Dylan wants to make a film
Called *Eat This Document*. Lennon doesn't
Want any part of this madness. Now,
Even now, he knows much crazy madness
Will come: Vietnam, various arrests, miscarriages, police
badgering, Yoko's love, lost weekends.
He has already been
On Ed Sullivan, at this point, and
He doesn't want to deal with a babbling, drunk
Bob Dylan, so he giggles nervously, and hopes
The camera will run itself
Out. He doesn't care if years later
Beatle fan-at-tics will see
Bootleg videos of him and Dylan stoned,
but he doesn't want to hurt the feelings

Of Barry McGuire, Johnny Cash. He decides
To let Dylan worry
About pulling his own foot out
Of his own mouth. In years to come,
When Dylan finally meets Johnny Cash, he will
Make a record along a *Nashville Skyline*. Lennon knows
This, and he further knows he won't be around
Much more than another 15 years. Still,
He recognizes greatness, and he realizes,
While sitting in the backseat, that there will be
A tribute, someday, to his old friend. Down
The road people will celebrate this skinny kid
With puffy, punky big hair and nasal
Twang. He's right!
Everyone has come. Tonight is very special,
And Lennon just happens to be
Back in New York City for a while.
He notices many people while wandering
Around backstage. In the distance
He sees a familiar face,
A stagehand who once got him
A guitar chord when he was so nervous
And so stiff and so afraid before
His 1972 benefit concert at The Garden.
Seeing this stagehand's familiar face seems to excite Lennon
In many ways more than seeing any
Of his old pop star friends
Behind the action, behind the music, there he is still
Doing his stagehand job, just as if twenty years had not
Passed. When Lennon turns his head, he is
Sitting in the tenth row-center, next to
a young lady who is the wife of a midtown business man.
She lives, happily, in Fort Lee, New Jersey, but tonight
her soul belongs to Dylan and to Manhattan. She has
Always loved Dylan. She remembers seeing him
Many times ever since his early 60's start
In The Village. As the lady contemplates her past,
Boos and bad spirits erupt and fly
Out like millions of dark sparrows. Lennon is confused.
He looks up to the ceiling and quickly to the stage.
He notices a bald-headed woman in the spotlight.
In an instant he realizes

She is the one feeding these birds. People whisper
Something about her inappropriate behavior
On national television. Lennon knows all about this.
He has made a similar gaff, several years ago.
He hardly ever uses memory this way anymore.
But he can't help but recall a teen mag interview
And a statement he made
By mistake. It cost him
What the bald headed singer must pay
For herself. She is forced to run off
The stage in tears. He knows, all too well,
That kind of pain and its hurtful consequences.
It feels like he and Yoko
All over again, and he hates that evil
Feeling, but it has been a long time
Now, and all the time is off the record.
His attention is, again, diverted.
He now finds himself in the cheap back
Balcony seats. He remembers Aunt Mimi, Liverpool,
Strawberry Fields, Julia, briefly in this moment, he remembers
The concert halls of late 1950's Britain,
And the best he could ever afford
Were the cheap-cheap-, faraway, back seats. Four guys
Seated nearby mention Eric Clapton's name, and Lennon
remembers
One late summer night in Toronto, Canada. He,
On stage with long, long hair, dark full beard
Holding beautiful Yoko while young, wired
"Slowhand" plays Holy Rock'N'Roll.
The crowd grows
Pleasantly still and they gasp.
Lennon sits
Stage left; he is attentive. He now senses loneliness
For the first time in a long time. He
Suddenly realizes this is why
He came here tonight. There,
In a purple jacket, is a youthful long-hair
With cherished, cherub smile. George
Harrison. Old dharma buddy who had made the journey
With John from Liddypool to Hamburg to 1962.
New Year's Decca audition
to the "toppermost of the poppermost" to America

To India to NYC, where Lennon's drained blood
Would evaporate outside
72nd Street and Central park West,
To forever. Tonight, young George is his wonderful
Friend. Lennon wants to tell George
Where he has been all these years,
But he doesn't know
Where to begin anymore.
Lennon wants to climb up
Onto the stage and sing
In old harmony spirit, but
Tonight is for George to repay his debt
To Bob Dylan for coming to George's aid
To help an old friend from Bangladesh to
Save his country, and Lennon stops
To meditate on the silly reasons why he refused
To show that night to honor
His English brother's request.
He remembers those different times
And those hard, different feelings
And they are all so difficult
To imagine anymore. George passionately sings.
Tonight his voice is like silk and honey
For Lennon's dreamy heart. It is
At this point that Lennon decides
Not to visit anyone else
Tonight. He thinks it is best to walk away
And to love time for what it was.
He wants to keep it all
Framed just that way. He is very happy
To see George up there shining
On and on. He is very pleased and fully satisfied.
He thinks that perhaps he might cry,
But he knows there are no more tears,
And, besides, nobody will ever know
That on a cool night,
Through a mid-October wind,
John Lennon came back
To New York City to pay
His own kind of homage
To Bob Dylan.

The Last Human Within

Miles from the centuries
Which claimed my presence,
As though I were
The last human within
The reach of a rattlesnake's tongue
Striking from the ear of a woman
Whom I knew once and
Whom I have known forever.
She calls me back
To an easier time:
Bathtub gin, Charleston dancing
Cars that were as new to people
As the invention of the first ballpoint pen
Must have been. Now, there are only tragedies;
Too many to count, too close to see.

I have suffered for the new year
As the colored lights of a fever rage
Within the darkness of the human hearts
Of the Native Americans who,
for century upon century, were stripped
Of all they owned: the dances, the land.
This America we now call
Our home was once only an "X"
On some explorer's map long ago.
The mourning chant of the Native American plains
Is the sound of an ancient instrument
Of loss. If we are being tortured today,
The pain will grow even stronger tomorrow.
The Chinese fortune of suffering:
"He loves you as much as he can,
But he can not love you
Very much." The struggle continues
Inside the Anglo dream. The snake,
The ink and the blood are the past
From which there is no peace to tie
Justice, like a ribbon, around our sins.
The southwest's reservations have more

In common with Beirut than with the American
Dream which is now just a lonely tale
Spun century after century
And from generation to generation.

I Have Found

for Bradley Jones

I have found
A pain hiding far
Below the nuts and bolts
Surface of my skin.

It stays dark
And away, deep within
The cavernous depths of my heart
Always beneath the horizon of my soul.

It wails and hurts
Continuous and committed
Driving me deeper
Into the facts of myself

And this world is a coward,
Frightened and scared beyond
Reason, muddled and clouded
By fear, anxious with awareness and desire.

I have found
A pain hiding behind the midnight
Of myself, and I will challenge it
No more.

Blue

for Lawrence Pike

The cold is blue,
Unexposed
Blood. Wailing
Through softly bruised
Memories.
Tender mercies that change
Everything.

Birth rewritten
On a transparent window
Shade.
That's you rolling up
tomorrow in the
Wind.

New futures always lay
Claim to investments that
No one
Wants to make.

Dogma

There are certain things that we believe
In that have been set before the slightest
Hint of ourselves ever entered
Into this universe of grace.

People everywhere were making plans
As we lay, quiet in our mother's
Womb. The fact that we may know
This was our place of birth makes
Nervous the authorities who conceived
Us. They waited in anticipation,
And when we arrived, they told us
Everything we would ever need
to know about this precious world.

When the answers did not satisfy
Us, and when our questions were better
Served to be left unsaid, the raging
Entropy began. It made them nauseated
To know that there were many
People just like us. People
Who couldn't exist in peace
Without the torture
And the hurting pain that truth can
Bring forth. Truth is
Our second birth,
And the parents in this world
Will have nothing
To do with your second passage
Through mysticism and into eternity.
So, mothers and fathers stand alone, present,
Forever, with their dogma. They stand
Howling in silence. Baying endless
At the children whom they may never know.
Newborn rebels, refusing
Their orders and challenging all
The light and all the darkness

Of the lonely world that continues
To weep as the adult centuries
Are little by little
Stripped bare.

Proverb

after Dorothy Day

The beauty of this
Life is so much
More than the world
Ever lets us see.

Brooding the Heartlands:

Poets of the Midwest

Save the Frescoes That Are Us

for Edith Parker-Kerouac

These murals would have existed here,
In Detroit, even if Diego had never painted
Them. The sweat and labor of this city,
Along with the sacrificed blood
Of its workers, would have stained
These walls. No matter what.

This town, beautiful, lonely child
Broken by too much post industrial
Hard luck, is always, once again,
Resurrected with deep convictions.
Our longevity cuts deeper than forever;
It's far longer than Rivera's Lenin headed
Murals-Rock Center-Manhattan, torn
Down by those city slicker liberals in NYC
Beachhead of American culture and civilization.

Not here! The politics of Detroit
Go beyond arguing fresco vs. classic,
Or any something vs. anything. Here we deal
In a culture of collective energies,
Beating union heart. Here, it's always
Work—Not talk. We know that
Talk is cheap, but work is
Forever. We know
That building is more
Essential to our survival than politics
Is to our reality.

Mass Production

When we look closely inside
The tunnel of the American
Factory, we see gears turning
In disorienting prophecy, it is not
Salvation that first catches our eye.

Diego Rivera said "Industry is
Our Salvation!" What he dreamed
Was a much different nightmare
Of wires and gears and smoke-
Stack lightning from the burning sleep
Deep within the cavernous factories
Of our broken hearts where we are left hollow
And alone on a cold highway
Of separation and pressing discrimination.

The American spirit has long been
Strangled at some untraceable point
Between the ideal and the real. Now,
We are hungry and we are waiting
For our justice to pass through
This system of mass production. The wheels
Grind slowly in a world of industrial darkness
Where the murderous dollar suffocates
Our hope with progress, and where
Our drams twist in fitful sleep.

Out futures lie stricken in
Inanimate blankness as we wait
And wait, like our ancestors did,
For a change that surely moves
As slow as blood through the thick
Grease heart of oil fed machines.

Straw Boss Dream

Hidden within the center
Of the industrial crush
Of oil, metal bearing shavings—
The American Dream
Drowned, breathless, stomped
Into hopelessness, strangled anger
The boiling pot of liberty blackened
By the greedy heart of elitism
And power. From a straw boss
Dream, we work to escape
The factory nightmares of lonesomeness.
Workers' souls are cathedrals
For harboring bruised labor, broken
Hearts and endless malaise. Alone
Our fear is work
Not "fear itself." Democracies
Are open market prisons
Where we all sell ourselves
Out to those who would
Otherwise rob us blind.

And She Left

She was the daughter of a sharecropper
Who left Tennessee for the loneliness
Of the Midwest. Under a sad urban moon,
She met man. A factory
Worker with a heart as rich as diamonds.
They married, and she continued
To work the land like kneading
The bread of her youth. Her emptiness
Was slowly filled with the mud
Earth, where she later lost
Herself, buried like the south
In the backyard of her past.

Where Are the Songs of Spring?

"ay, where are they? Think not of them,
thou hast thy music too"
—John Keats

for Allen Ginsberg

I have investigated the cryptic saxophone
Notes of wailing blues and desperate jazz.
Decoded them all into one long,
Wild barbaric yawp that I first
Remember hearing dance across the rooftops
In my neighborhood of silence.

The omnipotent shadow of nationalism
Followed me ready
To smother my dreams within
bomb-laden clouds of dying
America. The napalm nightmares of my youth.
I stood frightened and alone as America fell,
Realizing that no one would know,
Or hear the howling prayers of the young
Chanting endless Kaddish for the tortured
Burnt spirits of Hue, Mekong, My Lai,
The dried out Midwest: Chicago, Kent.

It was you, holy soul jelly roll, Bard-
Prophet who freed me, liberated us all
From our mysterious illusions of cornerstone
Backyards in suburban new America. I found
You—brother Poet—in the drowned coil
Of America's sleep. Where I, too, could not stand
My own mind. Where I, too, was not tamed
Or translatable. Where I, too, wanted
Only to come to the point of
Civil Rights, Viet Nam, CIA Death
Dance Politics, Dow Chemical Lament
And Plutonium Ode. I needed
To understand Che, Marx, Jesus, Buddha,
Beatnik, MC 5 stage rage, so that I could free
Myself from fitful McCarthyism doldrums,

143

And television eye snake dance. I needed
To understand that Fordism was fascism
To understand that Sacco & Vanzetti must not die
To understand that Father Ho was not our enemy
To understand that we were the wrong side
To understand that Malcolm X was right
To understand that America killed JFK, RFK, M. L. King,
Chaney, Goodman, Schwerner, Evers, Till, Hampton
To understand COINTELPRO's endless attempts
To silence Frannie Lou, Rosa Parks, Oches,
Sanders, Abbie, Dillenger, Berrigan Brothers, Cleaver
Newton, Seale, Savio, Davis, Steinem, Chavez
To understand that Lt. Calley was a murderer
To understand four dead in Ohio
To understand that for every city burned,
For every Wounded knee, for every Jackson State
For every homosexual murdered and persecuted
on the streets of America—
America could never be
Put back together again.
Allen, you understood
This, and without hesitation
you put your queer shoulder
to the wheel . . .
Lord, Lord, Lord,
Caw, Caw, Caw,
Lord.

Bass Beat Blues

The bass beat blues is
A supple tone alive
Across the surface of a jazz
Moon burning in the misty midnight
Hour. Flap, scat against the long
Cool neck of a polished upright
Sound, flash playing the hurt
And pain of the dark, ancient
Music into somewhere sound
That breaks like a heart torn
Wide inside itself. The aching
Beat bass blues pushes on
And on way out past
The setting evening stars.

Unaccustomed Mercy

For W. D. Ehrhart

There's something wrong with me.
I'm damaged. It's like something in
the center of my heart is gone and
I can't get it back.
—from *In Country,* Bobbie Ann Mason

Now, so many years later
And so far away from Perkasie, PA,
I sit in a classroom
At a major Eastern university,
And I listen to scholars
Talk too much
About you and your poetry.
But, my mind stays away
From all their academic, post-war babble,
And I imagine you as a young boy lost
In the American foothills of the Alleghenies.
Young, tender, but tough enough to be
The son of a preacher and a Marine
In the secret house of Viet Nam.

I think about your early days, alone,
In rural Pennsylvania, many miles away
From yourself and the tired love balled up
And clotted in your youthful heart.
I imagine you in a car full of care-
Free country boys drinking and running
An old beat-up Chevy down
Those same hills that built you
Up only to push you down
And out across an America
That would later break your spirit.
I wonder, now, about your confused high
School decision to run away
To the jungles of Southeast Asia.

I wonder, now, how frightened you must have been
Smothering all that fear in
Your angry, young lungs
Hiding in the mean streets of Hue.

I wonder, now, how broken
your mother's heart must have been
When she first learned
Of your school boy decision to leave home.

I think about your heart
And mind, the combination you gave
Away so freely—for mother, father,
Brothers and community,
But you gave away more—
You gave of your unknown self.

Now, Bill, all these years later
We are left with all of those awkward lies
That we continue to whisper to each other
To help us avoid reality. And we, like you,
Remain forever unaccustomed to mercy,
Walking endless patrol
Around the perimeters
Of our lonely national pain—
Awake in the blueness of our sins.
And, still afraid of the unrecognizable
Truth of Viet Nam

In Memory of the Passion Stars

This is how I will remember
It. A cold, dark Michigan night
As crisp as a new prayer, blue
Like the season's first snow.
Too early to remember
The children of winter
I never knew, coming back
From wars fought in my sleep,
Everlasting beyond the universe
Of my dreams.

And I shall spend forever
Worshiping all those eternal mothers
Who gave birth, but were forced
To believe that war is
Nature meeting history to resolve
The national loneliness of ourselves.

I am marking a calendar today
To make clear to all
That solitary spirits open
Everyday into every season,
New with passion flowing
Free and clear of anyone's
demands or anyone's
destruction.

America, beware
Of these cold, crisp payers
That will bind you
And recall all of your crimes
And hold you accountable.
You will have to answer
To all those eternal mothers
Whose passions you have
Drained
Endless.
Forever!

148

Detour Calamity

Tomorrow may be
Calm to the touch,
But the detour calamity
Of today has changed
Me forever. I can
Not turn back to the twisting
Wind weeping. Its eye
Has been swallowed within
The tail of the storm,
So I lie
Empty, waiting
For the quiet
just before the dawn.

Brooding the Heartlands

There were those days
Lonesome out on
The Dakota Plains. Lonesome
In my prairie rose daydreams—
Memories brooding across the heartland.

I remember wheat fields and wind
Conducting plainsongs through the wheat's
Chaffs. Bass tone husks—deep
Resonation out over the great divide.

I remember hearing, or thinking I heard,
The thunderheart lament of
The Native ghost dancers, moving
Their prayers, like heavy stones,
Away from the tomb of America.

Steal Yr Face Right off Yr Head

for Jerry

On partly cloudy, partly
Sunny days while seated lonely
Alongside train tracks
That seem to head deep
Into the heart of a midwest
Winter, salted with flaked frost
And cold bone chill—On
Those days, if you look
Close into the steam
From a locomotive's blast,
You can see tiny, thin angels
Trembling and twisting in
The smoke of the wind.
Almost transparent spirits
That seem to wave goodbye
To the passing trains,
Or are they gentle hellos
From faint, eternal hands?

Either way, they're too soon gone.
In the blink of one quick eye,
Just like the halo around
The head of a match, and you
Saw it too—even if you don't
Remember it. That's when you
Realize it ain't never comin' back.
That's when you start to feel
As hollow as a train's whistle
Vibrating inside the taunt
petals of a haunted desert rose
Hangin' sideways off
A tough cactus—solid—dry
As sand, yet as rich as a mirage.

Ancient Breeze

The soft breeze off
The lake blew the ancient trust up
From deep below the surface
Of my dusty shoreline neighborhood.

Fishing late into the night,
I bait my past,
With white-capped waves like
Wind inside the moon.

Boyhood classmates whom I had committed
To friendship in my memory
Flashed within the high tide
And angled just out of reach

Of the sunfish that are
Entwined forever
With my past and the future
Of the sea's retreating waters.

Caged

for Jim Wallis—Soujourner

Sometimes a poem can become
Like the gray-brown bark of a tree,
Clinging to the wet,
Pale Skin of the trunk.

Sometimes a poem can become
Hard and rough like the trees
Eco-outer coat that keeps
The inner veins fresh, flowing and

Hidden away deep within the darkness
Of the tree's secret lies that seem
To surround its beating pulp heart
Within each rhythmical leave and metaphor.

Sometimes poets want to push
Their poems upward through
Every tulip's petal planted
In the earth of the sun

To release the pale soul
Of every poetic line from
Within their tree bark grave,
To tell the world how

Strong and soft the soul
Of loneliness becomes
When caged within the specters
Of shade and shadow.

Written in Rain:

New Poems

Allen Ginsberg's Dead

I know Allen Ginsberg's dead,
And I want to write
A poem for him just like every-
Body else wants to do, but I can't
Help but think of my neighbor
Who too died alone, recently, in his home of
30 years, and how he was a person
Who will never have a poem
Written in his honor or to his memory.

He was a person who will never have
His life enshrined in sound
And symbol of verse or song.

I didn't know my neighbor either,
But I want to remember him
With verse and poesy just the same.

I want to celebrate
His life as the important treasure
He most have been as someone's

Husband, father, brother, friend.
I want to do this
Simply because he lived.

My neighbor wasn't famous,
And I probably only saw him once
Or twice in all the years that I lived
Behind his back fence.

But his words always made me
Amazed at the kindness of this world
When he spoke softly to me,
While he tended his garden.

I don't remember his words
As memorable quotes spoken
By a famous person. It was just small talk

Spoken in the lexicon of the backyard.
No "Howl" or "Kaddish" or
"Sunflower Sutra" to be sure,

But graceful words that rose
And danced over the fence,
Behind his red bricked house.

So, while I would really love
To write a poem for Allen Ginsberg,
Like everyone else, right now
It seems more important for me to capture
My neighbor's life, just another person
Whom I never knew.

I'll write it all down
In a poem that he'll never read
And that his family will never see
In print or hear at a public reading.

But, isn't that what poetry is all about?
Images speaking to the unspeakable
In our dreams as we lie awake in our sleep?

And, now, because I've shared this poem
With all of you, we are forever connected
All of our bones together
Side by side in the rich graveyard
Soil of poetry and life.

Pain

The Pain. It hurt
Everyone. It know no
Color. It start like a small,
Evil insect, and it enter
Thru those thin, small veins
In the soul. Thru the feet or
Thru blue edged vessels
In the fingertips. It crawl
Slowly, changing form along
The way from this to that. A person
Can see it some
Times by raising the skin
Up one hair
At a time.

The Source of My Liberty

Tomorrow the edge will appear
Far off in some distant cry that has been
Cut through wailing cliffs of horizon
Clouds that lie like smoke
At the ends of our lives.

Alone, I have wondered how
Many times the clock yawns
At daybreak. Or, if God's fire
Starts in our hearts as a process
To burn our soul free from sin
Now, in this flood of love, I remember

That once I was
A young boy before I was
Born, a simple life crawling in
An innocent twilight circle
Where all stars sleep
In the minute of a day.

I am wondering now if all
The anger I have ever felt
was really just my soul rubbing
hard against the blue metal trigger
Of my life. Now, I wonder if
It has all been a lie told
As truth in another
Universe—to forever obscure
The source of my liberty.

Tell Us of Life

*for Bart Giamatti, late Commissioner of Major
League Baseball & Man of Letters*

"I think we've done what we came to do."
"Which was?"
"To see if one inning can change the world."
—W. P. Kinsella, from *Shoeless Joe*

And when are you coming back
From your long, dead inning?
When will you bring your many
Stories home, conjure man?

You have stories of a world
On the other side of the diamond.
Out there far removed from
Everyone's lies, dreams, and breakdowns.

You are testing death
Now. A post season drinking
Of the ashes becoming its funeral
Of clouds, the father baseball of rain
In our childhood memories:
Easy, silly, foolish task.

And again it will be joy
To see you rounding
Tomorrow. With no uncertain
Brooding clouds to puddle up
And slowly bang and bang away
Our rhythms that'll wave us home
From beyond the changing
Horizons of our hearts.

Still, today some of us are as sore
As it gets, as tired as playing two,
And as sick of hearing all
Those playful, pitiful tales
About the rubber game that slid away.

161

Now, all of our days are shortened
By one, as our memories grow longer,
And we continue to toil in the outfields
of our youth looking for seeds
Of leather and stitch to grow our past
Up one more time, only to ease us
Back into the chalk-lined earth.

Marshmallow Dice

A spider in an old man's
Beard is like a marshmallow
Made from rolling dice spinning
Out of the world's cup of oozing
Volcano ash. A child at midnight
Is like a flesh baby in mourning
Appearing as a puffy cloud in
A simple glass of Russian Rosé.

I think to myself. Aloud.
If I wake before
I die, I'll witness
More eternity than most will
Ever hold in the palms of their
Hands. Love is only an open field
In the loafing, lottery sky.

Twisting Eye

That twisting eye, in
The heart of the wind, is me
Being whistled around
And around within the empty
Spirit grasping at grains
Of sand that are minutes
Representing hours representing all
The days of our empty souls.

Our Bones Together

for Rudy Baron

There is sadness
As dark as a suburban moon
Hidden, rural by nature,
Behind the blades of grass
That form the currents of our futures
And later the blankets of our graves.

We are all somehow connected
All of our bones together, placed
One by One
Side by side
Neatly within, the body
Of the night. Our skeleton
Horizons lie bare
Like silent bleached bones resting
in the grayness of the clouds.

The skull of the moon
Offers its light, mixing
The night with the mist of our souls
Stirring alone, blending together
The shadows of sadness
With the centers of our dreams and
Thrown beyond the twilight of all
Time and into the grace
Of our midnight hearts.

The Night Is a Loner

Sometimes, alone in the haunting
Moments of my dark, dark self, I am
Able to recall turns of panic, convolutions
Like high wind through the hollows of my youth.

Wind. This strange breeze I
Once grabbed and rolled into
Earthworms, good bait for catching
The twilight stars hidden
Beneath the waves of myself.

The night is a loner.
I have seen it asleep
And felt its sadness, clouds
Covering heat like pity, moving, stoking
The fires of burning anxiety.

Panic turning, creating wheels
In my sleep. I spend some time
Hoping for change, all the while
Twisting myself deeper
And deeper into the dark earth
Of the night.

Drunk

My turn is just like everybody else's.
I'm just another nightmare twisting
On a flagpole, paying my allegiance
To an unbridled, unsaved past.

The future keeps calling, but like a phone
Left off the hook, I've wasted
Too much time between connections,
And waited through too many years
Of bad wires and misdialed truths

Again, I push the buttons
of my life, and again, I am
Left ringing and ringing.

Realize the Noise

Once I realized the noise
Coming from behind was the turning
Of factory wheels in my soul, I leaned
Forward to place my ear against
The hot steel sun of lament.
I felt invisible, like a deck of cards
Slapping the wind's rubber face.
My reality.

Up Against It

From the city's sewer grids, I saw a soldier's soul
Vaporize up towards the slivered
Moon's chin. At that second, I
Realized that every moment of my life had
Only been an illusion, like a beam
Of darkness illuminating a midnight school of fish
Moving themselves out to sea along
The sharp edges of the moon's shadow.

Lake of Lonely Dreams

In the Lake of Lonely Dreams,
A fish is just another wave—
Another crashing illusion—hitting
Against the hardness
Of itself.

Seatones

Seatones murmur from a lonesome
Whale spinning through the blues
Of another life, rising up
To meet all of nothing. Nearby,
An air bubble whispers its memories
Of itself to nothing in particular.

With each breath, the soul
Of the ocean bellows in underwater
Earth sounds that unleash life upwards
Through a universe of salt and sea.

Soul, Deceit, Crying

It beats against
My teeth. Big sounds
Pulled from below
My soul. Deceit-
Cries roar out of my lungs,
A new life pink thrusting from deep
Within the walls of my mother's dreams.

The words were there
Even when I was not, but
I didn't know them enough
To speak. So I chopped
With my tongue, softness
On the roof of my mouth,
Splashing in vowels. A new
Food being pushed up
Through the tulips in my throat.

Still, in anger, I sit alone
Wondering which came first—the word
Or the tongue—thick sounds tossed
Onto the dark floor of my birth.

Nothing Is Real

Nothing is ever real
In October. The fresh
Angels of our past
faith dance themselves
Away into the winter's clouds
That will later back-
Pedal into our lives
Disguised as Spring.

Rereading America

America was never America to me.
—Langston Hughes

I want to reread
America. I want to
Rewrite history as my own
Hand painting my own hand,
Shadows of ink on a broken piece
Of stone that someone's left alone
By the side of a highway
Heading east away from here.

I want to redesign
America. Make it fit
Like a puzzled star
Into its burnt flag soul.

I want to tell a lie
As big as this country. A big,
Old lie that will shake
The whole world down to its roots
That have been re-planted
In the icy illusion spirit of our dead continent.

Somehow, I'd like to push reality back
With the same hard muscle of hurt
That America has forever, painfully
Carved into the generous hearts of its people.

Not Enough to Change a Thing

I stand accused.
Murder. In the basement
Of my sleeping soul. I let
Her slip out of my grip
Into the milky night of Heroin:
Dirty needles, yellow-tinted skin
Like a million canaries feeding
On her heart. Birds of death
With teeth like razors sharpening
The midnight moon's torturing
Twilight shadows that had always been
Secured tightly, attached to her future.

Her childhood slapped her face, red,
Every time she met the street,
Like an old friend that just can't
Be trusted. The neighborhoods challenged
And beat her time and time again,
Every single moment, like a bad memory,
Washed in the nightmare of her
Webbed, stained glass soul
Until she finally was forced
To lay down. Her burden
Heavier than all the love
She could ever muster.

I, now, must stand accused
For my own ego that allowed
Me to sink so far into a young galaxy
Of Heroin, a million stars
Around my future, lighting my way through
The darkness of death. My pupils, like her's,
were once small dots oozing life
Out, through the suicide
Of my own youth. As painful
As the letting go is
the holding on
To that which can cut you

Wide open and leave you disturbed
Beyond life. You see, I

Now must stand accused
For the murder of the future
Because I did so little and stood so silent
While the past pulled
Its shroud over the corpse of all
Tomorrows. I saw it all
Come back and down
Like the blood of the final
Letting go . . .
Of what and to where
I do not know.

Brothers

*Upon Visiting the Graves of Duane Allman
& Berry Oakley in Macon, GA*

*We lay red roses on his grave
speak sorrowfully of him
as if he were but newly dead.*
—Robert Hayden

They whispered one
To each other through the red dirt
"The road goes on forever . . . "
But I wonder now if that's
Always true? Could it really
Be this way, even on a hot
Macon summer afternoon
Stifling, sweltering along
Side the train tracked riverbed
That drifts upward above
Mushroom dreams and police siren
Gravesites filled with dirt and youthful
Peach Tree angst and motorcycle nightmare?

Long ago, in a Georgian night, Duane
And Barry played their last
Licks on a Southern Street
Mixing gasoline with pavement and blood
With cheers while Fillmore smoke
Rose only to settle back again
To eternal earth sleep beside a river
And rusted old metal train tracks.

I wonder how the mint leaves
And Jasmine trees smell
In the dark mud of death? Is there light
And electricity pulsing under cement cover
Of blackness, or does the road, now, seem
Open and full of the lonesome songs
Of yourselves? Today, at your graveside,
I make the sign of the crossroad blues

177

Over my heart—the only music the living can
Translate—a Southern chorus played
By the lonesome songbirds of death.
Their hum rising to sing up a new moon
In the black light night of slide
Guitar and bass blood thumps
Beating together—underground—forever
Like the blues trailing off the whisper
Of morning's breath—Just before the dawn.

Waiting for the Green Moon

for Peter Green*

I am waiting and I am waiting
For the green moon to rise
Above the din and smoke
Of this dank cosmic bar planted
Delicately in the dark forest
Of sweet scent magnolia dreams
And wafting winter pine, an incense
Offered to the blues heaven of my youth.
Transfigured soulful twelve bar, 4/4 beat rock'n'roll.

It is, indeed, a green moon
That has lit me tonight—Shone
High as a skyrocket shot up
Through the long neck electric
Music of old Willie Dixon's ghost guitar,
From behind once he said to me
"I know you," and gave a knowing smile.

Like a big broken heart mended,
My blue soul beats enlightened,
Painless love—brought together
At that right moment
When we all will wait
No more.

**Peter Green was the founder of The Fleetwood Mac Blues Band.
During the late '60s, they were at the forefront of the British Blues scene.*

Barren Tree Against Dark Sky

Children live in a very small world.
—Boston Globe

There are people with bad souls who leave us to die.
—12-year-old Albanian Child, 1999

Unlike anything before,
A child's face appears as a pale
Shadow etched into the starched
Gray clouds of another endless Serbian night.

The fire sky blends
Human image of face
With brown leaves of death
Amongst tall barren trees.

The metaphor of night is broken
Loneliness, a slowburn that takes
The soul deeper into the sacrificial
Heart of Blackbird Field.

All the children become
The kindling wood of their forefathers' agony,
Carved oak death mask of war.
No one hears or knows

How many will die
But the news reports the numbers
Will escalate as sure as the blackness
In the night moon's flames holds

More bombs echoing loudly
Off teardrop stars—falling upon
Balding birds of death—vultures
Feeding upon tender hearts

Of children who have been publicly
Beaten and humiliated in camps
Then paraded through the mean
Streets of American fascism and greed.

On the radio, a lonely girl
Says "I want to paint all the things
Of Kosovo, so I don't forget
What the bombs will destroy and burn."

It hurts us all to look at more
Bad history in another land of misery
And feel the pain that feeds the Blackbird
Ghosts who hide amongst the barren trees
In another pitch-black Balkan night.

Sitting Shiva for Janis Joplin

For Alicia Ostriker

We started all over
Again, taking it from
The top while driving
Through a crystalline midnight
Of another dark Michigan winter.

Stars as pointed as bright laser
Musical notes hung above
The universe of the sky. Cold
As heroin outside, and blank warmness
Inside, we listened close to each
Street blue lyrical poem
Of Janis'. We were driving

And sitting Shiva for Pearl,
Me and Alicia talking
About our raging rock'n'roll mama
Who was filled with the spirit
Of Mother Bone Blues wrapped
Between a Ma Rainey twilight
And a Billie Holiday dawn.

With her picture turned inward
Toward the walls of s'n'roll automobile,
We tore at our sleeves and chanted
Endless Kaddish and Christian prayers
Knowing Janis was in our sadness
And in the loneliness of each musical note.

Off a distant mountain, we heard
A coyote cry from out under
The blue jazz nighttime skies
For just one more sweet chorus
And one more holy refrain
Of dem ol Kozmic Blues.

Dakota Chapel

For Kathleen Norris
Spiritual Dakota Friend

God gave poetry to us
As a far reaching peace
From within a small, white-bricked
North Dakota chapel. Set high
Upon a wind-blown hill, perched
like a dreaming angel,
Waiting to heal all wayward
human pride.
In quiet church corners,
Tucked into every angle,
Are precious hymns that forever
Resonate with deep and silent care.
Angels' wings float out with each
Breath to release their reverence for
Our Lord.
This is the land where the Old Ones knew
Life as a whole . . . one circle of faith
Created under a red-gold Sun—Holy
And Sacred.

Under Construction

Upon Visiting St. John the Divine Cathedral in New York City

This cathedral is a huge heart
Beating under the tender
Skin of the Holy Spirit.

There's true light as a beacon
Pouring necessity through sweet stained glass
Architecture: corners and crevasses filled
With soulshine lighting every turn.

Radiant cathedral heart of comfort,
Tender, be our quiet place
For the loneliness of simple rest
From the spiritual weariness of this world.

Soft hues of love drape
Their beauty across alters of charity and grace.
Each page of scripture a blessing sung in love
Passed easily through the melodic, pink lips
Of the angels of all hope and liberation
To settle into the fabric of ancient church history.

One long, rich story of truth
In the word made flesh alive
Within those same walls that have absorbed
Century upon century of pain from millions
Of distrustful congregations twisting
With the human sin of non-commitment.

O Invisible spirit of love
Reveal Yourself here,
Before every person inside, and out,
To make known that something wonderful
Is alive inside, under candle's light,
Song and reverent prayer. Our hurting,
Changing hearts transformed
By Apocryphal Psalms—Whispered,
In mercy, to the rhythms of our hearts.

Against Sunrise

The sun raged wildly
Against the horizon as
She sat silent on a beach watching

Horses race across the red sand
Over glass shadows in the distance—
That appeared as though God had

Lain a carpet of love
Atop a mirage of a lonely desert.
She sat as still

As a tongue frozen
In mid-sentence at dusk.
She gazed casually at falling

Water drops dripping off
Ocean petals of time—wet and alive.
She felt the movement

Of climbing to heaven
On a ladder of fat clouds
Propelling her upwards
Into a great joy beyond
The angels of her past.

Burning Like a Monk

For Norman Morrison

As simple as an overflowing cup
Of inward meditation waves,
The mind closes and opens
For nothing of importance
To anyone.

We wonder if we are
Someone or just some-
One's imagination that has been
Cultivated in the dry garden
Of self-righteous purity.

Some have spoken, throughout
The decades, of the simple flames
That have danced upwards
From the backs of prayerful
Monks who had been
Set afire and lined up in rows
In the streets of our past wars—
Constant flames
Of unforgiveness and sin.

Their humanity, as burnt offerings,
Serves to remind us of our own
Denial and destruction. We have
cemented our souls of sacrificial
Toughness to the tortured necklace
Of death that we will forever wear
Heavy around our thick necks
Like an anxious memory
That won't let go.

Tender to the Bone

For the late, great Dave Dixon

So, here's where
We are now.
Our friend gone,
Turned to ash
In a nighttime
Of purple sky.
Shades pulled one
Last time to
The edges of
This cruel world

The music of
His last breath
Played softly away
From his room
Full of Mirrors.
Alas, broken in Spirit,
But still tender to
The bone of
Love. He knew
The rhythms—he
Had them deep
Within, and now
He takes it all
To the next world.
Alive in melody
Where all things
Dance forever under
A mirage of pain
And of light.

Going, Going, Gone

It's the top of the end.
—Bob Dylan

For Ann & Ken Mikolowski

After the sun has passed
Over the last flower
In the final meadow,
We will understand how love
Has connected us all full circle.

The days were once
Endless with love, filling
Our cups in the city
Of our youth where we tended gardens
Of romance and art—where we touched
And moved from one body to the other,
Easily from within our deep souls creating
All that was ourselves.

We all knew then that someday
We'd have to separate to leave this world,
But we now know that someday
We'll all meet again over yonder wall.

Out where our love will reign
Supreme forever and endless,
Where our lives will once again be
Returned to each other—
Together alas and always.

M. L. Liebler is the author of several books of poetry including *Stripping the Adult Century Bare* (Viet Nam Generation Press), *Brooding the Heartlands* (Bottom Dog Press), and others. Much of his work appears in national journals, magazines, reviews and anthologies; his performance poetry, with The Magic Poetry Band, appears on CDs, cassettes, and albums. He was a poetry correspondent for CBS Radio in Detroit and hosted his own literary program on public radio. Currently, he is the Detroit Director of The YMCA National Writer's Voice Project and the Arts & Humanities Director for The YMCA of Metropolitan Detroit. He has taught literature, creative writing and Labor Studies at Wayne State University in Detroit since 1980.

Typefaces used were Nimrod, designed
by Robin Nicholas; Michelangelo,
adapted by the P22 foundry from the
handwriting of the artist; and Baker
Signet. Bitstream's Venetian 301 was
used for credits and the colophon.
Type was set by Alan Berman using
Corel *Ventura*.